Boxology

Boxology

Thinking and Working Inside, Outside,
and Beyond the Box and the Cubicle

Irving H. Buchen

ROWMAN & LITTLEFIELD
Lanham • Boulder • New York • London

Published by Rowman & Littlefield
A wholly owned subsidiary of The Rowman & Littlefield Publishing Group, Inc.
4501 Forbes Boulevard, Suite 200, Lanham, Maryland 20706
www.rowman.com

Unit A, Whitacre Mews, 26-34 Stannary Street, London SE11 4AB

British Library Cataloguing in Publication Information Available

Library of Congress Cataloging-in-Publication Data

ISBN 978-1-4758-2132-1 (cloth : alk. paper) -- ISBN 978-1-4758-2133-8 (pbk. : alk. paper) -- ISBN
978-1-4758-2134-5 (electronic)

∞ ™ The paper used in this publication meets the minimum requirements of American
National Standard for Information Sciences Permanence of Paper for Printed Library
Materials, ANSI/NISO Z39.48-1992.

Printed in the United States of America

Table of Contents

Preface   vii

Introduction: Boxology: Innovation Environments   ix

Part I: Boxology Dynamics   1
  1 Outsmarting Ourselves: Ten Ways of Devaluing Innovation   3
  2 Box Variables and Dynamics   7

Part II: Profile of Out of the Box Types   11
  3 Difference of Out-of-the-Box Types   13
  4 The Two Faces of Talent: The Upside and the Downside   19
  5 Talent Management: Marriage or Mismatch?   23
  6 Talent Isolation: After the Honeymoon Blues   27

Part III: Innovation Advocates and Strategies   31
  7 Problem Collaboration   33
  8 Innovation Prep: CEO Conversations   43
  9 Innovation Advocates, Enthusiasts, and Evangelists   49

Part IV: Innovation and Integration   57
  10 Innovation Range: Three Professionals and Their Process
     Preferences   59
  11 Training and Taming Trouble Makers   67
  12 Innovation as Convergence   73
  13 Future-Embedded Innovation Methodologies   85

14 The New Species of Boxes—Think Yourself Out of Those!   103
15 The Policy Box   105
16 Advocates for Innovation   109

Preface

Does every one inside the box think the same? No differentiation? No evolving levels? Then too, where do those who think outside of the box, go? Back to the original box to go through further iterations? Not likely; after all, they have outgrown their box. Like Adam they have tasted the fruit of knowledge and they are banished from the box of Eden. What happens to them? They fall into history and evolution. Each generation reenacts the drama of their thinking birth and emergence from the fetal paradisiacal box. Each one is doomed to further—perhaps endless –development. Each one is blessed and cursed forever with restlessness—with endless curiosity—and with the haunting memory of their original and archetypal release from the box of limited thought. But in the process they also leave behind a number of puzzling even enigmatic questions to wrestle with:

1. What are these outside and outside-the-box people like? What are their characteristic traits and behaviors? Who employs them? To do what ? Do they remain compulsively innovative?
2. Is there any historical pattern or, better still, myth other than that of Eden that would provide a deeper understanding of the recurrence of their original intellectual birth and ongoing developmental journeys?
3. What kinds of mentors and environments initially and subsequently best encourage and stimulate their original release from the box and their later intellectual development and innovation?
4. What corresponding new habits of the mind do the talented begin to cultivate to preserve their innovative edge and productivity? What happens, for example, when the focus changes from "How smart am I?" to "How am I smart?"

5. Will these talented and innovative professional in the process create new cognitive models of future thinking; and if so what are they likely to be? All innovation is ahead of its time; in fact, it is embryonic: when innovation appears so does the future.

The answers to these and other questions are the burden of this book. But before we get to all that we first have to deal with the basics—the strange foundational art and science of "Boxology."

Introduction

Boxology: Innovation Environments

Before automatically recommending everyone to think outside the box, perhaps we should pause to examine first the nature of the box—"boxology"—its forms, behaviors, and of course its thinking. And not just outside but also inside the box as well? Happily that focus will trigger a number of different and more disturbing kinds of questions.

Why are we in boxes in the first place? How did we get there? Was it voluntary or involuntary? What kind of thinking goes on inside then box? It had to be OK for a while but then it was evidently not good enough; because we are then asked to think outside of the box. But we really don't know what that is.

And what happens when we leave the box? Where do we go? Into other boxes? And what happens to our old boxes? Are they recycled? Finally, is there a method to all this madness? Behind it all is there after all a management system of boxology? How and why did it all start? What are the design options or variables of boxes?

There are three: size, shape, and substance. Exploring the apps of each may answer many or all of the above questions.

SIZE

Boxes order and contain. They organize the world and us. They are good for us. But they are not one size. They come in small, medium, large, extra large, and sometimes for CEOs, extra-extra large. We all start out as small. We are more manageable that way. We also are more obedient. We also discover that small requires nearly total compliance; loyalty remains always an absolute. Size may vary with range of responsibility but performance and obedience remain permanently paired.

We progress through size. Understandably the bigger we are the more space or the larger the cubicle we require; some even come with a door and/or a window. The CEO corner cubicle has both. Size is thus correlated with position. All boxes above and below are in turn held together by chain of command. Our thinking is similarly shaped to be hierarchical, linked, and reinforcing.

The basic thinking inside the box is the same in every box .The goals are the same: productivity, efficiency, and profitability. When it works, over time it becomes the culture of the boxes. "This is the way we do things around here" becomes also "this is the way we think around here." Success locks in and binds both together in uniform affirmation and in the process recalls the wonderful old folk song about how we all build ticky-tacky boxes, live in ticky-tacky houses, create ticky-tacky communities and work at ticky-tacky jobs.

The point is obvious: we love our boxes; we love talking ticky-tacky. We can't think our way outside the box because our thinking is boxed. The fault lies not in our thinking but in what contains and imprisons it. We mistakenly believe that freeing our thinking is only a cognitive rather than an organizational problem. All we have to do is invoke the magic of talent management, hire the best and the brightest, and all will be well. But unless and until talent and environmental management are made one, we will be putting Einsteins in boxes. Indeed, if all these new hires were as bright and creative as hoped, they would resist your on-boarding box and begin to share their insights and knowledge of boxology. And if you did not listen, they would leave.

And leave you in the lurch? Of course. But how bothered would you be at the loss of such talent, how aggravated by the general difficulty of attracting such innovative types in the first place, and what paltry record of innovation would you have to show for it? Finally what would it take to goad you into exploring experimentally another design variable?

SHAPE

Boxes teach a number of lessons. The most obvious is you cannot outgrow them. Big VIP boxes are just as stifling. Then too you cannot exceed them. You can't be smarter than your box. That in fact is why the call is to think outside rather than to improve your thinking inside the box. Finally, even if you had the experience of eureka, it would be regarded as a fluke; the euphoria would be short lived lest it become a new norm or expectation. The boxes would close ranks and the nail sticking up would be leveled by the hammer box.

But if what is sought is genuine and total change—if desperation and enlightenment and not necessity are the mother of invention, then innovation ends require innovative means. What should be involved then is not just thinking but questioning what kind of shape our thinking is in.

Begin with introducing other shapes: specifically, circles and networks. Boxes are containing, circles are enclosing, networks are extending. Boxes are hard and inward facing. Circles are soft and inclusive. Networks are rubbery and linking. If boxed in, circles and networks would go limp, lose their shape, and lose the energy of their difference. Compromise is not possible. Boxes are too tyrannical.

Circular and network cultures are essentially horizontal not vertical. They tend to be free flowing, informal, boundaryless. Ideology has not hardened into orthodoxy. It tends to be a noisy place; in a hurry; often unintentionally rude, smart-ass, no-holds-barred, and witty. In contrast boxes are boring.

A circular bull pen leads to more collective than singular outcomes. Networks are reinforcing and encourage not only more collaborative relationships but also a network identity. In a circular and networking culture every one is both an Indian chief and a brave. It is a tougher but kinder environment. It is more demanding, self-reliant, self-evaluating. Goals are consensual and never exceed your grasp; and if they do, their achievement is shared. It fuses competition with mutuality, tough love with affection. Job satisfaction is ruled by reciprocity; my satisfaction involves and is contingent on yours. Finally, certain absolutes have to prevail: no mean-spirited rules, no gotcha games, no tantrums, no anger, no fits of indignation, no punitive and arbitrary personnel policies and above all no bullying bosses. They are all the enemies of innovation.

Sounds idyllic—too good to be true? But perhaps our skepticism is embarrassing? Are we not affirming the inevitable reality of boxes? Are we so stuck that we cannot imagine not just thinking but enjoying a different kind of existence outside of the box But before throwing our hands up in despair, let us add one additional utopian element: substance.

SUBSTANCE

So far we have not considered what our various containers are made of. Boxes are solid closed in, and dark. Circles and networks are more open. Whatever boxes are made of they are stronger than we are. Besides, changing the shape would be costly; we would lose what comforts us. Circles invite relationships—a more flowing set of relationships. Rectangular tables compel a head and an end; round tables are more playful, accommodating, equalizing and even democratic. Although some may lament that no one is in charge, mystical advocates of the form claim the circle is in charge. If circles become too rigid or exclusionary, they dry up, atrophy, and become old before their time.

Networks introduce negotiation and conflict resolution. Circles and networks complement and fit each other. In teams they operate in tandem and seamlessly to generate innovative problem solving. In conclusion, given the clearly open, even-handed and nonauthoritarian nature of network circles, it seems obvious and appropriate that the substance of our new culture has to be made of transparent plastic.

In summary, then, our failures to think outside the box are instructive. They point to generating expectations that elude fulfillment not because they are impossible but rather are a mismatch of individuality and mutuality, competition and cooperation

In other words, they lead us to boxology and the laws of containment and liberation, size, shape, and substance. What becomes clear is that we make culture; and that when the goals change even radically we can remake culture. Thinking inside the circle sometimes can match, replicate and even exceed thinking outside the box. Then we no longer will we ask that you think outside the box but instead that you think inside the circle. Because then you will have the best of both worlds; the comfort and protection of containment and the liberation of thought and creativity.

Part I

Boxology Dynamics

Chapter One

Outsmarting Ourselves

Ten Ways of Devaluing Innovation

Sorry to begin negatively but when it comes to innovation there is more to lament than to cheer about—more examples and apps of non-creativity passing itself off as the real thing—and so many self-imposed, self-limiting attitudes—that we have to clear the fields of obstacles before we can move on.

Worst of all it is self-inflicted.

But for generally smart professionals to be so regularly and easily outwitted and deflected suggests collusion—evidently we have bought into a number of self-deceptions. Thus, surprisingly, even the reasons for being outsmarted are not so much accusatory as exonerating. But unless and until we understand why and how we are lulled into innovation myopia and complacency, the road less traveled will elude us and we will be future-less.

There are at least five attitudinal reasons why we are blindsided about innovation.

1) Company Durability—("We don't really need it.") If your company has been around for a long time, survived market ups and downs, and your products and services have remained household names, then it is not unreasonable to assume that all will continue to exist and even flourish without the intervention of innovation. To be sure, a great many companies in the past operated under the same precarious assumptions and disappeared. Extrapolation generally is not a reliable guide in a changing and disruptive world.

2) Customers—("Our customers love us.") Your customer base is solid and loyal. Getting repeat business does not involve a hard sell. Attendance at annual company bashes is exceptional and high spirited. But if you look ahead, you find that the demographics are changing rapidly and dramatically. That does not mean that customers will become fickle and look for something new. You think: "We do not have to change. Time is on our side. Let us wait and see."

3) Employee Training—("We are current and cutting edge.") Happily, we have routinely upgraded and updated the workforce .The net result has been high levels of competence and alignment. Then too, we have just introduced mobile e-learning, serviced 24/7 by our website. Of course being current is not the same as being proactive. In fact, strangely, the former even often obscures the latter.

4) Continuous Improvement—("We are always breaking new ground.") This commitment ironically is the most illusory. It gives the false impression that innovation is at work. But shaving a few hours off the production schedule or shortening the lag time for customer complaints is incremental not discontinuous—a management strategy not a Eureka process.

5) Hiring Innovative Talent—("It is sometimes a gamble, and often backfires.") Two obstacles immediately surface: defining such talent and positioning the odd balls in the company hierarchy. The results so far? Expectations have been greater than achievements, grass-roots creativity has been discouraged, and personnel dislocations abound creating often a management nightmare.

The five factors above are powerful persuaders that innovation is not needed, or worse, is already going on. In either instance precisely the companies that should be hearkening to the urgent sirens of disruptive technology are listening to the lullabies of the status quo.

But sticking our heads in the sand is not limited to deflective attitudes. It often stems from and is built into our organizational and operating structures:

6) Upper Levels Have the Smarts—The pyramidal structure enforced by the chain of command tends to limit leadership and new ideas to the top or upper levels. Rank and file is generally excluded. This puts enormous pressure on a minority to perform—again and again. Then too, the chain of command makes them nervous and worried about what their supervisors will think of their new ideas—not the most encouraging environment for creativity.

7) Creating Different Comfort Levels—There are two extremes: the comfort of continuity and the threat of end games. But, perversely perhaps, innovation does not thrive on either. Rather it is disturbed into being. It comes alive in disruption. Why? Because that is what innovation is—a disturber of the peace—a disruptor. The delicate task is to replace inhibiting comfort levels with more durable levels of uncertainty that are not debilitating—to nourish and tap the natural kinship between order and change on which innovation feeds.

8) Excitement of Vulnerability—As noted earlier the tendency is to emphasize success and put a smiley face on all. But innovation is not a happy camper. It is not likely to happen when the guys are having a drink after work. Innovation is serious but not grim. It does not fall apart but is braced and challenged by bad news. It rolls up its sleeves and quickly proceeds into problem defining directed by the diagnostics of company vulnerabilities. The focus, then, should be to compile and tally risks. Overall continuity is not assured. The search is for the weakest links; for review of recent decisions which increased vulnerability, no matter the trade-off benefits; for company change that exacted a future price. It is often the little things that can undo you. The micro can disturb the macro; the law of crash is slip.

9) Big Ideas—The Eureka Moment—Many companies and especially their leaders are into visioning and the big picture. Obviously there is nothing inherently wrong with that. Indeed it often has driven organizations to new heights. But frequently such goals are predicated on producing great breakthrough innovations that leap frog the company way ahead of its competition. Although that sometimes happens, history favors many smaller, less sensational examples, which also tend to be more easily absorbed, implemented, and marketed. There is always danger of putting all or too many eggs in the same basket.

10) Who Is In Charge?—The answer takes us again back to structure, whether it is highly centralized or distributed. The former favors the few because they are clearly accountable for the power and favor granted to them. Typically with innovation it is R&D and the talented—indeed, that explains the current obsessive recruitment and separate management of talent. Generally, the talented are not put in cubicles; indeed, many have doors and even windows. But their principal distinction is not as lone rangers but team players. As team members and leaders they bring team performance to new collective and collaborative heights. In addition, in the process of working together they have successfully identified many creative members of the rank and file never before singled out or recognized as innovative. Indeed, as result of both initiatives the talented have bridged top and bottom—the two cultures and structures.

In summary then innovation is not limited to producing new products, processes and services but has the power to change both external and internal structures and rejuvenate and build excitement and confidence in the workplace and among the workforce. It is the kind of impact we expect only from leadership.

A law of escalation operates in forecasting. The future is offered in three forms: stretch, strain, and shock. Not looking ahead combined with decision paralysis surrenders options. What was initially reasonable but forsaken (stretch) gives way to the grim (strain) and finally to the draconian (shock).

The imagination is thus always an endgame. Indeed, it often begins with terminus and then in brooding fashion takes us back to genesis—to where we went wrong. But what we fail to appreciate is the extent to which the apocalyptic imagination is also analytical; and further, because its scope is total and inclusive it is finally also interdisciplinary.

But in the process, history never totally abandons us. It puts in our hands the means to comprehend the future of the future. But hopefully this time to arrive at a new leadership point where sustaining replaces controlling; where managing replaces dominating; and where vulnerability, excess, and myopia, properly addressed, can transform the utopian imagination. And such transformations are always the task of the trinity of thinking, talent, and innovation.

Chapter Two

Box Variables and Dynamics

Many find it difficult, others impossible, to think outside of the box. Why? Because for most of us far from being limiting or inadequate, being boxed in is comforting and reassuring. Everyone is in the same boat-box. It insures mutual understanding. How else could we communicate so effectively? Boxes talk to each other. They look for and find other boxes that are mirrors of each other. Remember the old folk song that described how happy we were to build and to live in ticky-tacky boxes and create ticky-tacky families and ticky-tacky communities?

Boxes are mind mirrors. Our thoughts reflect our identities. We all live in boxes. We all talk ticky-tacky. For better or worse we make peace with our lot and our contents. That in turn determines the degree to which we resist or hearken to the call to think outside of the box. And yet, surprisingly, given the power of that content to affect stasis or change, we have generally neglected the identification and analysis of the nature and range of such mental states. Instead we issue unilateral orders to change and wonder why we don't—not recognizing that there is not one but a multitude of boxes lined up in a sequence of evolution.

Minimally, here are five kinds of mind—boxes:

1. "Mind-Blank"—innocent, original, a tabula rasa. The desire for comfort and quiet is so strong that it embraces and is absorbed into a permanent fetal twilight zone.
2. "Mind-Lock"—the most rigid, lockstep, cocksure box of all. It is absolutist and tyrannical. Although as single-minded as Mind-Blank, it is ideological, committed to a cause. Trained by various drill ser-

7

geants, it can't wait to be given its marching orders to prove its un-swerving loyalty and total obedience.

3. "Mind-Set" put in place and programmed by cultures—familial, soci-etal, company and national—and therefore the most guiltless, exoner-ated, shared, and loyal box of all. Most subject to time, decay, age and birth order.

4. "Mind-Mix" is a historical repository of all prior box states housed, archived, and coexisting so as to be available to retreat or regress to as needed. Rejects all accusations of being indiscriminate, claiming in-stead that it is the supreme eclectic, open to wizardry and hard science, revelation and horoscopes.

5. "Mind-Flow"—sometimes called Mind-Flex resentful of hierarchical structures and their compulsion to rank and pigeonhole. Fiercely inde-pendent and revolutionary, it impatiently seeks only systemic change. Aware of being boxed but recognized also as being exceptional and superior—on top of its game, up high and high up, the best box of them all—voted the one most likely to think outside of the box. But beware of opening this one; it may be a Pandora's box.

Stepping back and taking in the larger picture, what do these boxes repre-sent? What do they have to look forward to? Gazing around, what do they see? Down, alongside, and up—an endless pyramid of other boxes, and on top, even a CEO box. The incessant call to escape by breaking free is thus juxtaposed and even opposed by the prospect of jumping out of the frying pan into the fire—exchanging one box for a better-paying one or higher up. But is that progress or duplication? Better off staying where you are—con-tent with the familiar box of your current mind.

All organizations are built of boxes—at least five kinds. Each box is insular, sealed off from each other. Each level has the same distribution; and thus miniaturizes all. But taken as whole, this mental version of the organiza-tional chart may have unique value as a source of operational insights, cor-rections and conclusions.

First, it serves as a scanning and assessing device to generate critical profile patterns of personnel. Thus one can survey all middle managers and find in the process more mind-flow than mind-blank or mind-lock boxes. In other words, the proportions of each not only vary, but also hopefully tip the scales toward the side of those favoring out-of-the-box thinking.

But such in-house analytics are in turn contingent on recognizing the variability of the essential building blocks in the first place. Assuming wrongly that all boxes are the same boxes or have no differentiated content prevents and precludes companies from discovering and capturing the mirror of their internal makeup—of assessing that all-important distinction of pro-portion.

Second, operating on one-size-fits-all also jeopardizes training focus. The net result is singular audience definition and the predictable sputtering or blurred effects of missing the mark. Similarly, once the ideal or optimum mix is determined then the span of mind-profiles can define and guide not only mind-liberating strategies but also recruiting criteria and targets.

Finally, we are left with a number of wonderful questions. How did the boxes get that way? Is it genetic or learned? What percentage of each? Are they evolutionary? Can we conceive of each stage as an upward progression in a Maslowian manner? Finally to what extent do we accept mea culpa, our share of the shaping of the mental boxes? Are we like the Russian nested dolls, the biggest box of all being company culture—the box of boxes?

Part II

Profile of Out of the Box Types

Chapter Three

Difference of Out-of-the-Box Types

First a corrective: are they all superstars, geniuses, members of Mensa, holders of Phi Beta Kappa keys? Some are; that is inevitable. But the evolutionary and representative stakes are too high and tough for innovation and creative thinking to be elitist. In fact, on the contrary, the egalitarian, across-the-board efforts of exceptional professionals in all fields and disciplines are needed. Otherwise the evolving intellectual models would not be in fact models—generic, representative, and persuasive.

At the universities these outstanding performers would be dubbed the best and brightest; in business they are now designate as the talented. But all share the same strengths:

- They are unfinished—initially, permanently, and finally.
- They operate with no sense of limits imposed from without by past or present generations.
- Nothing is impossible.
- There are in fact new things under the sun.
- They have a strong sense of their difference and of the road less traveled.
- They are productive loners but equally strong team members.
- They are self-managers, requiring little or no supervision.
- They also have the capacity to be self-transforming even self-transcending.
- They eschew offers of leadership, preferring instead be part of a collective effort to create future versions of human intelligence.
- They are superb problem solvers, but ultimately they create solutions that are unique, futuristic, and elegant.
- All innovation is ahead of its time.
- When innovation appears the future appears.

LINKING DIFFERENCE TO TALENT AND INNOVATION

First, a few up-front assumptions: not all differences are alike; not all are good or nice; not all surface early, obviously, or painlessly; but all finally converge as a definitive predictor of emerging talent and leadership.

Not so fast. What do you mean by difference? Is it the same as uniqueness? If so, then you may have inadvertently just thrown out the baby of transferability with the bath water. Then too, what are the special dynamics of difference that not only mark current talent and leaders but also foreshadow those of future? That "difference" predicts emerging talent is a major claim for something you have yet to define, Clearly, more explanation is required before our opening assumptions can be accepted.

Granted; so below is a ten-point taxonomy of the characteristics of difference:

1. Horizontal Base

The classic question raised about leadership can be applied to difference: are leaders born or made? Is difference innate or acquired? And the answer to both questions as well as both their parts is the same: "Yes!" But that in turn requires reframing the issue of genetics versus the environment.

Difference is a product and function of the interplay between nature and nurture. But nature and nurture are not opposites; rather, they are two sides of the same coin. They do not compete but share twin versions of each other. They are not controllers but secret sharers of a common evolving identity. Throughout, the mystery of definition and of its evolving interplay thus remains a permanent constant.

"I am different because I am both programmed and educated to be that way. Without the permanent interfacing of my inherent talents and learned abilities, without their frequent and unpredictable cross-overs, I would be ordinary—always less than I could be—distant from being talented or a leader. I would be summed up by 1 plus 1 equals 2 instead of 3."

2. Vertical Extent

Because not all difference is equal and not all differences are the same, differentiation has to be introduced. Horizontal equanimity requires the supplement of vertical hierarchy. Otherwise there would no accommodation to the two ruling principles that govern both nature and nurture: the diversity of the species and the standards of the survival of the fittest.

Difference thus obeys the rules of variety and differentiation. Although The talented are never equally talented or talented in the same way. Preference is historical and societal and is driven by the changing values of the age, which directly in turn affect the standards of hierarchical evaluation.

3. The Dangers of Excess and Presumption

An identity that is not set or final but evolving operates independently as a stream of consciousness. As such, it feeds upon itself, has a will and direction of its own, and can become a law and world unto itself. It can become convinced it is infallible; every problem will be solved brilliantly, every executive decision will be perfect. The preoccupation with origins and ends can create a heady almost cosmic series of performance expectations to the point where difference believes it can never fail or model exemplary behavior.

There are thus two great temptations. One is becoming self-sufficient, the other is becoming infallible. The two fold into each other to become a mutual quest for a superior place in the pantheon. But when difference shows its true colors and turns its penetrating analysis on its own potential excesses something magical happens: the pursuit of immortality is transformed into the pursuit of singular excellence; and the desire for perfection becomes the passion for innovation. And both these in turn become the gift of fire wrestled from the gods, but now delivered as a mortal model for the followers. The emergence of talent and leadership thus reenacts and affirms the process of evolution and creates the standards of getting there.

4. Composite

Difference is not a single strand but a composite of interwoven traits. It has to be that way because the weaving together is identity creation. In addition, such intertwining accommodates not only an almost infinite number of individual variables, but also defines difference ultimately and finally as an amalgam. Being a composite not only constitutes a unique distance from others, but also largely accounts for the solutions of synthesis characteristic of the talented and executives.

5. Community of Differences

Talented people and leaders have no difficulty identifying each other. Indeed, that frequently takes the form of noting and being curious about the differences between their differences. Thus, contrary to conventional wisdom, the society of the talented is not exclusive but inclusive and brings together and creates unexpectedly a community of common differences. Each one is equal in talent and leadership to all the others but some are always more equal— first among equals.

6. Discovery

Sooner or later—better sooner—difference has to engage in self-recognition. Sometimes we are surprised into it. We take charge and do something dramatic and someone inevitably says, "He is a born leader!" Or you solve a difficult problem that has baffled all, with ease and without bravado. Suddenly all step back in silent admiration.

Gradually you become aware that there is something different about you. You had a sense of it before, but now it is being externally noted, confirmed, praised and valued. The discovery of your difference is the major event in the evolving and interweaving process and fixes you forever to yourself and to the distinctive journey of your talent and leadership.

7. Rejection

The discovery and acceptance of difference is such a powerful and affirming experience that we cannot imagine how else it could be treated. But sometimes the response is not affirming. It depends on what it does to or for you and how in turn it allows or directs you to shape who you are.

You may find that your difference is embarrassing and backward—that it sets you apart, and you do not want to be set apart. And so, defensively, you hide or mute your difference as if you are ashamed or have to apologize for it. Such suppressed difference puts you at odds with your potential and sadly makes you less than you could be. As such, that disqualifies you from being considered talented, not only because the talented are never ashamed of their talent, although they may be humbled by it, but also always seeks being more than they can be—especially in the characteristic holistic and integrated way of talent and leadership.

8. Twisted Rigidity

Even more surprising and at the other extreme, is the difference of a singular rigidity that thrives on being set apart. We are not accustomed to linking difference and intractability or egotism because we tend to regard difference essentially as benevolent or neutral. But difference can be an intense form of single-mindedness—of a compulsive personality who has a determined and preconceived drive to achieve a certain kind of success, salvation, or sainthood. Thus, we are not talking here about quirky or fragmented behavior but a tyrannical insistence on only one prescribed way of doing things, and of following directions without question: "It's my way or the highway. I did not hire you to think. I do all the thinking around here."

Difference is used here to produce an almost military display of precision and competence paraded before the visiting generals. Although outwardly impressive, it is at a lesser level of talent or leadership because it is coercive.

It sadly produces the bullies, lousy bosses, dictators, and martyred coaches who always say to their teams: "We stand out. We have standards. We are superior! We are different!"

9. Putting Difference in Charge

The talented individual is neither ashamed nor excessively proud—the talent is just there. But what is critical is putting difference in charge and not making any decision that would diminish its contribution or centrality. In the final analysis, when difference chooses, it always chooses and affirms being different—what has made the talent what it is in the first place and what it will become in the last place. But that choice is not made once and for all time; it constantly haunts and revisits you, especially when the question arises of whether it is all worth it and imagining what it is like to be ordinary.

10. Difference and Innovation

Difference never leaves you or leaves you alone. It is your shadow, your secret sharer, almost your spouse. Difference is both origin and evolution, genetic and environmental. Difference is talent and talent is difference. Both are obsessed with their mutual desire for embodiment.

The talented are innovative because of the way they sense things, people, and problems. Nothing is ever familiar or occasional but a unique, onetime, nonrecurrent, and one-of-a-kind event that may never occur again in precisely that combination. Thus immediacy is prized because it is more open to and ripe for talented access and inventiveness. The talented come up with the new because they regard each puzzle as being as different as they are. It is a one-of-a-kind experience for both. It has to be that way so that the discovery is mutual and reciprocal—binds problem and solution together in the common ecstasy of "Eureka!"

PROFESSIONAL AS POET

In summary, we need only recall the classic expression of Robert Frost's "Two roads diverged" to understand the point of life and career change. Talent always chooses difference—the road less traveled. That is the less popular, predictable, sensible, and advantageous road talented people always choose—or more truthfully, it chooses them. Even though it carries with it two burdens: being sentenced to a lifetime of being a poet—not a novelist or journalist—and being an advocate for a road that is disadvantaged and divergent.

In this sense, all talented professionals are really poets—happy and doomed to convey the same message of being permanently unfinished—the final characteristic of difference.

GOVERNING AND INFORMING NARRATIVE

What drives these creative thinkers? Their quest is not like or summed up by the heroics of Prometheus or Daedalus; the talented are not that rebellious or presumptuous. Rather they are more like Faust, whose pact with the Devil enables him to become a chameleon, assuming all sorts of shapes, smarts, ages, and roles but whose power is conditional on his remaining permanently unsatisfied. If he would ever say of the passing moment that it was perfect and he need not seek another, then the Devil has him—so it is with the talented.

The argument here is that the talented serve as our avant-garde. They are inevitably anticipatory; they rehearse and play out future images and forms of the species. Meanwhile, the Devil is on the sidelines cheering them on to the failure of contentment.

Chapter Four

The Two Faces of Talent

The Upside and the Downside

There are three standard tests to determine if a new field is to take hold. It has to be needed, to attract followers, and to be institutionalized. Talent management clearly qualifies: it addresses serious shortages; engages specialists in many disciplines, especially HR; and has acquired its own journal, organization, webinar series, and annual conferences, In short, TM has arrived and flourishes, and yet some of its assumptions remain unchallenged and even unexamined.

The most critical one is that there are many downside behaviors of talent that make its management difficult and sometimes impossible. Indeed, that analysis and its findings question the efficacy of talent management altogether: namely, whether talent in fact is manageable or whether it even should be. In any case, a sample of five talent traits are listed and described below in two dimensions, the upside and the downside.

1. DRIVE

Upside

Talented professionals generally exhibit high energy, enthusiasm, zip, and motivation. They never invoke job descriptions as jurisdictional, turn requests down, or refuse to do their share. If they are ever hesitant, it has nothing to do with commitment but rather their pondering how to do the task. Typically they are keen and eager about their work: show up early, stay late, and come in on weekends to finish assignments with tight deadlines. In short, they are exemplary models of drive and dedication.

Downside

Talented employees know how quick and good they are, especially compared with their coworkers. They also have rated everyone in the unit against them selves. The problem is they seek early recognition and promotion, and are not willing to put in the conventional time to earn either or both.

2. SMARTS

Upside

Talented professionals are bright, quick, sharp, eager learners. They grasp big concepts easily and often apply them in unexpected ways. They love to argue and problem solve, although often too ingeniously and tenaciously. Their hands go up first in training sessions. They seem to be on a perpetual steep learning curve and are little upset when their coworkers have not read the latest best business books.

Downside

There is a difference between being smart and smart-alecky. Unknowingly, they are like peacocks parading and dispensing their superior knowledge and insights at meetings and training sessions. Often nervy, they are the only ones who question whether the emperor has any clothes on. One manager observed that often they were too smart for their own good. But that does not stop them.

3. STANDARDS

Upside

They have high standards. Quality is their god. They reject fast and dirty, all shortcuts, all cutting corners. Always follow letter of the law. The customer is the absolute measure of all. Ethics call all the shots. In fact, some are hired and assigned as corrective models to units notoriously sloppy, slavish, and sluggish in their work standards. Finally, to the talented there are no limits to performance quality. If there are, then the limits are those of the company not the talented professionals whose aspirations never exceed their grasp.

Downside

They are too absolutist. Nothing is ever either black or white. Everyone fudges a little, adjusts margins, claims more than is totally true. That is the ay of the world: padding and under-the-table deals—you scratch my back and I will scratch yours. But such operating realties of their coworkers do not deter them. They remain self-righteous, challenge every process, and create a conflictive and nervous work environment. And no one is wiling to take them or their principles on.

4. INVENTIVE

Upside

Their constant question is why do we have to do it this way? That is followed by the familiar mantra to think outside the box, repeated so often that one comes to regard that call itself as knee-jerk and boxlike. Today's talent knows how fashionable and desperate we are for innovation, and they play to that audience. And when every once in a while we hear the cry of "Eureka!" the pace is intensified and the entire rank and file is asked to be similarly creative The notion that anyone can be president has been switched to anyone can be Thomas Edison.

Downside

In the process, the slow and laborious traditional way of incremental improvements has gradually been discredited, minimized, and sidelined to clear the way for speeding sensational innovations. Meanwhile, talent has been invested with the mantle and role of rescuer and savior of the economy, while every one else bears the burden of proving they are equally creative.

5. AUTONOMOUS

Upside

The talented love their cubicles. They love to be by themselves and to work alone. They need no supervision. They are a manager's dream: "If I only had five more like him, I and my unit would be on easy street." Their reports are always handed in on time, free of any errors, well written and organized, and finished with due diligence. No one comes close to matching their output or quality. The talented professional is a world unto himself, a one-man band, a productivity center in his own right, and a supreme loner.

Downside

Being solely a solo is not the model we need to follow now. Teaming is what is needed—collaborative learning, cross-training, a culture of mutuality and reciprocity—that is what is being called for. The days of the Lone Ranger are over, although we still have to contend with that image as an obstacle.

In many ways the two-dimensional profiles above are no surprise. No one ever claimed that the talented were nice or that it would be easy and routine to manage divas, the brilliant, or a herd of cats. But at least we are more aware not only to what extent their difference is innocent and inherent, but also the impact of their behaviors on less talented coworkers and an on talent management itself. In other words, talent and its singular focus have changed supervision altogether and shifted management from personnel management to the management of interpersonal impacts, doubled. The upside and downside are now no longer aberrations but new norms, and no longer limited to the talented but now inclusive of the entire workforce and environment. The final impact is double doubling.

Talent management not only has increased significantly our understanding about interactive and interpersonal management in general but also has generated a series of insights into unethical operations, lack of standards, naked CEOs, and perhaps most devastating of all the organizational limits that the talented encounter . To ignore all that would dramatically signal the failure of the talent retention policy and even the final loss of what it struggled so hard initially to recruit.

Chapter Five

Talent Management

Marriage or Mismatch?

In a relatively short time, talent management has secured a significant and highly visible place in the workforce world. Although only a few may bear the explicit title of talent manager, it has become a standard and regular update to many job descriptions. HR has not only eagerly embraced but also championed it. It sometimes commands a separate and substantial budget item of its own. Of course, technology has had to demand its piece of the data pie and generate the numbers to insure the validity of measurement control. Finally, it has become its own field; signaled by acquiring its own journal, webinars, and annual conferences at which awards are given and the gospel is spread.

And yet for all that, is talent well served? Do we really believe talent can be or should be managed? And is talent better for it? Does it perform at higher levels and is it easier to retain? But lest one conclude that such questions are a prelude to critiquing the mechanics of existing systems or a platform for proposing a totally new one, what is involved here is neither. Rather, the call is for a more basic, back-to-square-one approach. Specifically, we need first to describe what makes talent talent, and then determine what it needs to function at an optimal level—and whether it benefits from being further directed, managed, or institutionalized in any way. In short, we need to view talent in and for itself—its essentials as well as its operation in the workplace.

The following are five such generic characteristics of talent:

1. *Presence.* Talent is always recognizable, sometimes immediately but never obviously. Talent prefers a low profile. It does not seek to call attention to itself. Even its dress is neutral, blends in. Its presence is quieting and reassuring signaling the entry of competence and the intention of being there for the long haul. Even when transferred to another unit or team, the same pervading aura of quiet professionalism carries over. All feel a bit more confident and even eager. Talent thus typically brings a palpable difference, a little uplifting magic to a routine environment. When the total is greater than the sum of its parts, the extra is what talent brings to the equation.

2. *Focus.* Talent is seldom small or petty. It has no tolerance for BS or sucking up. The talented find such behind-the-back antics degrading and demeaning; besides everyone sees through it. The talented person is not a prude or a loner; often joins the joking around the water cooler, but usually is the first one to get back to work. Loving work, talented people love to work with those who also love to work. Sometimes they come in early and stay late. Their notion of the work ethic is to do whatever it takes to get the job done, on time, on budget, and within specs. Their reports always meet deadlines and are never sent back for correction, amplification, or revision. Many professionals are workaholics but not all workaholics are talented.

3. *Bright.* Quick study, first time around. Able to grasp whole systems, preserve contexts, recognize and value variables. Always on a personal growth curve. A tireless question machine; asking why again and again with the dogged insistence of a six-year-old. Their strength as problem solvers is inextricably linked to their ability as problem framers. And all is pursued with due diligence; after the bike is assembled there are no parts left over. Their biggest frustration is limitations— not their own, because they know what they are and what they can do to overcome or minimize them—but the built-in, unacknowledged, secret limitations of organizations, per se. Often they are tempted to call out, "The company has no clothes!"

4. *Surprising.* Just when you think you have figured them out and pegged the key behaviors of the talented, there are disconnects. Suddenly and unrepentantly and contrary to prior interest, there are a number of sharp political indictments vehemently delivered; and then, just as suddenly, like the passing of a thunderstorm, all is back to normal. Or when at a team meeting a chronic complainer is about to launch into one of his familiar invectives, our normally respectful talented personae steps in and says: "Don't hold back Carl. Tell us what you really think." All chuckle, even Carl. And happily, Carl does not speak. Finally there is the quick wit: "That plan has the subtlety of a bull

dozer" or "He is a giant standing on the shoulders of dwarfs." Talent is never predictable or finally knowable.

5. *Productive*. Talented people get things done, all with quality control—no excuses, no delays, no late deliveries, no customer complaints. And the volume of work pushed out is equally impressive. The key to such productivity according to our talented professional is threefold: smart and agile systems, constant maintenance, and intelligent anticipatory market management. And of course it cannot go without saying: having talent in pivotal positions in all three areas.

Although the above list could be longer and other characteristics added or altered, talent emerges as formidable, indispensable, and independent. Equally as important, it is self-motivating, self-teaching, and self-leading—and finally self-managing. The only ones who could try to manage such behaviors would have to be equally talented, and their attitude and management style would have to be minimal to the point of being invisible

Such talented managers would have to practice benign abandonment, generally leave them alone; or if you must, keep them on a very long leash. Let them wander, go off for a long time without asking for permission, allow them to drop in at any time to see you without an appointment or subject. Above all, always be prepared to be surprised.

One supervisor related this story: "At one recent regular weekly meeting of the unit, our talented member stood up and suddenly and unexpectedly singled out a coworker for his native talent and the collaborative intelligence of his problem solving ability." In the heavy silence of admiration that followed, all, but especially the supervisor, recognized that no one could have managed what just took place. It was an extraordinary act of collegial kindness matched by the unique ability of talent to do what run-of-the-mill managers generally cannot do, and in this case did not do: use talent to identify talent—the ultimate sign of self-managing.

Chapter Six

Talent Isolation

After the Honeymoon Blues

Exchanges between HR reps at conferences and annual meetings always serve as a wonderful information clearing house. In the space of a few short days one can learn about the latest HR trends, pick up tips on some exciting company experiments, find out what everyone is reading, and of course hear the latest gossip about so and so and this and that. But of late there have been some disturbing and new rumblings about our newest and one of our most successful ventures: talent management. And the warning sounded is that if you want to continue to enjoy ROI then quickly and proactively put in place PYI (Protect Your Investment).

What do the major concerns and emerging problems seem to be? Warning: data is thin, anecdotes are abundant, and the issues are all over the map starting with the talented themselves.

LONERS AND ELITISTS

Talented people generally think highly of themselves and like who they are. They believe that 95 percent of everything is not first rate and their superiority is statistical and genetic, not personal, even though they have chosen to be official members of MENSA. They prefer their own company to the point of being dangerously self-sufficient. As a result, they cherish the role of the Lone Ranger rather than that of the team player.

Productive loners, they enjoy working by themselves, are good at it, and require little or no supervision. If left on their own, they would not be unhappy, and would continue to produce quality work. But as loners they seriously affect the morale of collaboration and jeopardize team problem solving. Ultimately, they give the impression of aloofness and elitism.

ISOLATION

Understandably, talented professionals are assigned to positions and functions throughout the company in appropriate units. But after having met a number of their talented colleagues at onboarding sessions, and learning of other new appointments, they may lament their structural isolation and being cut off from those with whom they have a special affinity and with whom they would like to converse. They are particularly puzzled why no one recognizes the problem, no solution has been found, and no one at the top has been an advocate to bring them together, regularly or occasionally. They sense conspiracy.

MANAGERIAL ATTITUDES AND BEHAVIORS

Many supervisors are not overjoyed to have these specially talented additions to their units. They are fearful that they might upset the happy balance that they have worked so hard to build over the years. Other managers may be suspicious that perhaps it is a negative judgment on the way they run their department. A few believe the newcomers are spies. But many are generally uncomfortable about these brainy types and inexperienced geniuses or divas. It would be easier to lead a herd of cats. Acting on these insecurities and biases, a number of managers have designed some questionable ways of welcoming their new talented recruits.

ILL-USED AND EMBARRASSED

The talented do not seek separate special treatment. Nor do they lord it over others. Above all, they do wish to be regarded as superior or cast as geeks or freaks. Given all that, imagine their reactions to the following: One supervisor scheduled meetings, led by the new star, on how ordinary people can be creative. Another designated the new addition as the principal go-to resource for help with problem solving because he was so bright and the only one who had an office with a door. Finally, one supervisor sponsored an early-morning breakfast of coffee and donuts for many units so he could conduct an interview on how one becomes talented and how to make sure everyone knows it. (Pity whoever is in charge of talent recruitment.)

SURPRISING ROLE OF THE TALENTED

In one case when interviewed and surveyed about relations with their co-workers, the talented all noted that they do not have a monopoly on talent. Typically they said, "I do not know if the company knows it but they have some very talented employees." Pressed further the criteria given were impressive; native intelligence, sense of systems, big picture, savvy implementations, often inventive solutions, questioning mind, pluck and grit, and so on. Also agreed upon was that such talent is independent of education, academic credentials, nationality, gender, or age.

Many of the unrecognized or under-recognized confessed that they went underground. Many were labeled as overqualified. Older employees were passed over for promotion for lacking academic degrees. A few aspired to managerial rank but were regarded as too allied to rank and file and not tough enough to fire fellow employees. But in spite of all the limitations, neglect and stigmas imposed over the years, our perceptive experts on the talented were able to cut through all that and in the process identify unexpectedly an internal network of talent the company never fully realized it had.

Finding such a treasure house was not what motivated the talented. Simply discovering and being able to work with such natively intelligent co-workers was sufficient. It also would never occur to them to see themselves in future roles of indispensable catalysts or mentors. They reached out an inquiring hand with no preconditions. So much for elitism.

So in summary what do we have? Obviously a mixed bag, but two patterns stand out. The first is the perception of the talented by all; starting with the talented themselves, HR, trainers, managers, and rank and file. Evidently, those in charge of Talent Management have been so excited by their new heady venture on the one hand; so absorbed in the difficult task of recruitment on the other that the need for preparing the way was not invested with sufficient importance. But now that sin of omission of forethought requires correction, which minimally involves providing basic orientation training for managers.

The second issue is equally obvious. Retention requires not data monitoring but keeping your ear to the ground, gathering bits and pieces of anecdotal evidence, and above all keeping track of stories of the talented not only identifying but working with previously undervalued coworkers. That last effort not only accomplished what no one else had, but also in the process expanded and raised to higher levels of performance a previously untapped network of companywide talent. That alone should drive and stir all retention efforts to keep what was so hard to get and what has provided from an unexpected source such substantial added value.

Part III

Innovation Advocates and Strategies

Chapter Seven

Problem Collaboration

Problem solving epitomizes process. Although the forms have evolved over time and vary from industry to industry, its basic direction and character have remained the same. All problem solving displays the ritual of a military operation. The problem is positioned as a target to be defined, surrounded, and finally subdued. Tactical support is provided before and during by a data system that contributes to precise problem definition. The methodology selected is usually tried and tested and associated with similar successful applications in the past.

Indeed, its recurrent application and rate of success not only may elevate the preferred problem-solving mode to the level of a best practice, but also may define company culture as well.

And yet, although many current problems and decisions appear to be more intractable and resistant to current treatment, our standard approach remains aggressively unidirectional, basically driven by a masculine command stance and system. Perhaps, an alternative and supplementary approach that should be explored and welcomed is that of problem collaboration.

Problem collaboration is based on three positioning changes. First, the problem solver is no longer the sole principal player or activator. He or she now occupies the periphery as the problem moves to the center. There thus is a basic exchange of roles—subject and object exchange positions. The problem is now in charge.

Second, the role change in turn involves another repositioning, as the subject, the problem, is now the talker and the problem solver now the listener. What takes place is no longer one-sided. It is not solely a monologue but a dialogue. The new relationship between problem and problem solver is now essentially collaborative and takes the form of an evolving scenario.

Third, the problem is personalized—through a series of prompts, the problem is asked the following questions:

- Why are you a problem?
- To whom?
- Big or small?
- Affecting other units?
- How do you present or manifest yourself?
- How would you define yourself?
- Any deeper connections?
- Are you new?
- Or been around in somewhat different versions?
- If we solved you before, what was the solution?
- And why did you decide to come back now?
- What would we have to put in place to get rid of you once and for all?
- Finally, since you know so much about yourself what is your solution to you?

Because problem solving is often a team process, final interaction requires that the responses noted above and collected separately by each be shared and consensus sought. That process not only multiplies but also disciplines the variety of perspectives into a more unified and manageable range of solutions.

Given its own unique voice, each problem would thus define itself, establish the benchmark criteria for its solution, and finally whisper its solution to those who listen closely and deeply to what it has to propose. In many ways, this is typically not what is done.

In many organizations when a new dubious policy or solution is unilaterally announced, the typical response is "If they really wanted to know what to do and how to do, all they had to do was just ask those who do the job."

Turning to the problem for answers is in effect a variation on seeking an expert solution. And if in the process our egos may be somewhat diminished or eclipsed, we should find consolation in that our problem-solving lives and operations have become more interesting, less predictable, and more open ended—and further, that this new symbiotic relationship is finally of our own choosing and for our own benefit.

Many organizations often characterize their missions and operations by their preferred methodologies: Deming's Continuous Quality Metrics, Six Sigma, Balanced Score Cards, etc. Even subunits may embrace a preferred protocol: HR may elect Talent Management, Strategic Planning, Trend Banks, or R&D Innovative Training. Moreover, how an organization and its problem solvers confront complexity may be heralded in fact as its competitive edge.

The way a company manages itself, optimizes its workforce, and navigates through often hostile environments is often driven and defined in large part by the state of the art of its problem solving. Organizations stand or fall, secure a future or fail to, largely because of the way they process problems. And yet, although corporate identity is often largely synonymous with problem-solving processes, we often fail to grant the mode the centrality of reexamination and perhaps reinvention. In such a case, best practice perhaps may be ironically and unexpectedly inhibiting and limiting.

But if successful, why change? Because a significant percentage of the problems we now face are not familiar, recognizable, classifiable, or docile. In other words, they are not just new and different—that is to be expected—but they appear to elude current calipers. They exhibit an unfamiliar profile:

- Time: future-imbedded
- Space: global
- Scope: ecological
- Rate: rapidly discontinuous
- Shape: holistic
- Access: systemic

And yet when the favorite problem solving methodologies of the past are obediently called on and applied to such often unique intransigence we are surprised by the mismatch. A new kind of tough complexity is greeted by past-driven processing with the result that we are regularly coming up short. Here are a few of the tell-tale signs:

- Misdiagnosis—we are missing the mark.
- Non-holistic—passing off halves as wholes.
- Root cause—we are solving effects not engaging deep/hidden causes.
- Not 360—we are singular nor interdisciplinary.
- Mechanical—knee jerk, obedient and uncritical applications.

Such shortcomings are bad enough but what is worse is that the search for what went wrong is confined to making sure that the problem-solving process was followed to the letter of the law. Talk about due diligence gone awry! What other courses of action might be considered?

The most promising is epistemological, because it challenges how we think, how we learn and how we know what we know. Abstract and theoretical and yet precise at the same time, this emerging development banks on new knowledge from

- brain research—how we learn, best,
- cognitive science—how we think, critically,

- multiple intelligence—how we are smart,
- innovation—how we are creative.

Although the implications for not only problem solving but also training may be far-reaching, we are not there yet. But while we are waiting for the emergence of those research findings and tests of their validity and reliability, there is perhaps a more mundane and immediate approach to consider. And curiously it comes not from business practices but from science fiction.

DIAGNOSTIC SCENARIOS—NEW VISIONING TOOL?

Why is looking ahead so hard, especially now? For at least three reasons. First, CEOs have more information than they know what to do with, partly because much of it is incoherent—unconnected, unintegrated, and often even conflictive. Second, on top of that, members of their executive team (often from the same generation) mount their favorite hobby horses and press forward with their chorus of future warnings, urgencies, and priorities.

Politics, which at this critical decision point should probably not come into play, regularly rears its jockeying head and revolves around not whose ox is gored but whose voice and view has most access to the executive ear. And finally, strategic planners, echoing members of the board, call for taking care of current short-term business problems while taking on the longer term—for present and not just future viability.

So what is a CEO to do? Where should he or she turn? One suggestion is to develop and apply diagnostic scenarios. What is that? It is a fusion/hybrid methodology. From the outset it puts together problem solving and forecasting, decision making with its projected reverberating impacts, solution and positioning—in short, leapfrogging. While we are catching up and taking care of present business, let us also try to get ahead. It also functions as a screening process: identifying and defining those problems and decisions that are not familiar or run of the mill but that strike terror into a CEO's heart because they imperil survival and because they are in bed with a discontinuous future. What's involved? Minimally, five steps:

1. Problem Scaling. Who else has this problem (of talent shortages, profit margins, global competition, etc.)? What have they projected as its future impacts? What is its extent? Industry-specific or does it cross sectors? Regional, national, global? Is any company immune? In other words, is there anyone who does not have this problem? What does the case study research show? Finally, is the problem like the proverbial iceberg—bigger and more entangling and hidden than we

thought? And is it solvable once and for all, or will it continue to plague us for years to come?

2. Future Scaling. Did we ever have this problem before? And if solved, was it linked to a particular future that in effect shaped, eased, and welcomed its solution? Or are you claiming that this problem and its troublesome future are new? That can't be. There is nothing new under the sun. Check the index of all the leadership books—it has to be there in one form or another. Otherwise we, like everyone else, are in uncharted waters and are not sure where to go. Is this what they call a paradigm shift? And are we already at that intersect? Is the world really flat after all?

3. Problem and Future Fusions. Take both the problem and our business on a time journey. Develop three scenarios—one predictable, one terrible, and one wild card. Dump the problem and our business in each. What happens? Do we survive, grow, disappear? Is the problem still around but we are not? Above all, does the problem have a future? Does it persist? Is it tenacious, long term? Or has it morphed before our eyes into a lovely butterfly of opportunity or assumed the menacing shape of a hostile acquisition or merger? If we are still around—in the same business—what do we look like? And am I still around?

4. Globalizing Contexts. Are there different cultural, nationalistic, even ideological ways of solving the problem and projecting the future? How would the French, Germans, and Russians go about it? The Japanese, Chinese, the Indians? Do they each have different futures that make their problem-solving processes more effective, less timid, more long term? Are we prisoners of our short-term quarterly fixation to such an extent that it determines not only our focus but also our inability to fuse problem and future solving? Suppose we were to outsource or subcontract our problem to the Danes or the Chinese; what would be the result? Would it be better than what we come up with? Would they also have difficulties? But not the same ones? Are we stuck in our traditional strengths?

5. Innovation: Fused Solutions-Futures. The ultimate end result of diagnostic scenarios is creative exhaustion—when all the tried-and-true strategies turn out to be tired and jaded platitudes, when our standard visions fail to engage and even pale before a future that does not welcome us, when we experience the throwback of being a start-up, and when in desperation we hear the familiar call: think outside-the-box. Piece by piece the problem-solving and visioning tool box is emptied, and we find ourselves not at media res but at genesis—not being asked to add another chapter but to craft a new creation story.

Diagnostic scenarios thus minimally offer three gifts. First, the methodology defines the new box we are in so that we don't reproduce or take it with us when we change vantage points. Second, it signals crossroads, paradigm shifts, and the imperative of innovation. Third, it develops the ultimate test for defining innovation as the creation of a new business that never existed before.

The final vision posed, then, is to become or incorporate that new venture, armed now with the knowledge gained by diagnostic scenarios that if we don't, someone else will, and in the process perhaps put us out of business.

In America we now sadly are preoccupied with endgames and losing the lead. We therefore need new tools, MBA programs, and executive teams to fuse problem solving and strategic planning, to bridge and manage discontinuity, to recover our future, and to support leaders who use diagnostic scenarios to integrate innovation and vision.

HORIZONTAL PROBLEM TRIAGE

It has become increasingly fashionable and predictable to call for outside-of-the-box thinking and to make such creative applications a training staple. To be sure, old issues still plague implementation: Should it be across the board or selective, a generic overlay or personnel-specific? Of late a new pressure has been added: to what extent should innovation be included and assessed as a determining factor of recruiting and hiring? And finally, what in general supports innovative company collegiality and culture and thus reinforces training and HR?

Although the answers to all the above may require extensive consideration, what is clear is that the subject of innovation has the capacity to break open and take us to the heart of program array, workforce performance, team collaboration, and organizational structure. But why? What about innovation grants it such centrality? Makes it so pervasive, inclusive, and invasive?

The most obvious answer is that it has become the make-or-break, do-or-die factor. Innovation thus emerges as both villain and hero. On the one hand, cutting-edge competition globally is so fierce that not only has market share been invaded and redistributed, but losing the lead altogether is a real threat. On the other hand, as a countermeasure, innovation has been called upon to rescue and renew vision.

The test of every genuinely new and creative idea is that it can become a business, sometimes that of your competition, who will be better at it. Innovation thus has not only changed the rules of the game, but also upped the stakes to winner-take-all. For some companies, the lack of innovation sadly has become the sign of its slide into an endgame.

As a result, innovation is no longer perceived as an option but a necessity, no longer a limited and singular factor but a major driver of everything, especially survival by leap-frogging. But there is at least one other perhaps more mundane but no less basic reason for the centrality of innovation: it epitomizes process.

Process permeates every organization. It is its distinction. It is what sets you apart. It is your competitive edge, your secret weapon. For many it even serves as corporate definition—"we are now totally a Six Sigma or Balanced Score Card operation." As such, it is proudly introduced at the orientation of new hires as your brand—as the way we do things around here.

Worked up as companywide rituals affecting and managing every unit and all personnel, it is ubiquitous and colors and leaves its defining stamp on everything. But precisely because process is so pervasive, the introduction of new ways of thinking, doing and managing, imparts to innovation both the opportunity and the threat of total access.

Thus, the first consideration is that the call for innovation may be potentially overwhelming—initially too totally demanding, too all at-once—for training to manage especially if it is across the board. Perhaps a bridge needs to be put in place between the old and the new ways of doing things—especially if we are persuasively to wean personnel away from the tried and true to the experimental and the new. Not throw out the baby with the bath water but instead mix the familiar and the different, what is reassuring and what may be stretching. And finally should we not practice what we preach by being somewhat innovative in how we construct our standard workshop on critical and creative thinking?

One approach is to begin by making all more scalable and manageable—by creating a process taxonomy, in this case that of problem profiling—identifying and classifying problems so that they can be matched with appropriate problem-solving methods. Such a taxonomy would identify where innovation is appropriate and where it is not. In effect, the workshop would be a series of exercises in problem triage.

The key assumption is that not all problems require creativity. Many are routine and familiar. With little or no fuss or adjustment, they obediently can be trotted through standard processing. Indeed, one could apply the famous Pareto rule of 80/20 to problem identification by claiming that 80 percent of all problems are essentially run-of-the-mill and only 20 percent are exceptions to the rule. It thus makes little or no sense to burden the everyday garden-variety problems with the heavy-duty and specialized focus of innovation.

But it does make significant sense to train all to discern the difference so as to achieve better matchups. The decision of who to train now takes on the more informed and productive form of training everyone in problem triage but not necessarily everyone in innovative problem solving.

But for the 80/20 rule to be a workable first cut, it needs to be followed up by what in fact defines each. How do we tell whether what we are dealing with is a problem that is routine or an exception to the rule? In short, what determines and triggers bringing in the big guns of innovation? Although what appears below is not designed to be definitive, it may offer a number of essential criteria not only to separate the wheat from the chaff but, more important, using the contrast to define what is not manageable by current calipers.

Although a number of processing screens could be cited, the three below can function minimally to sustain problem triage. In the process a double-edged sword is applied so that defining the differences between ordinary and exceptional problems is constantly a parallel and mutual activity.

1. Definable. Is the problem describable, recognizable, and classifiable? Does it exhibit and replicate familiar and recurrent past problem profiles? If different, are those differences of degree or of kind? If the former, then what adjustments can be made? And when the checklist is completed, the problem then can be dispatched to an appropriate solution ritual. But turning to the flip side, is its definition elusive, tricky, almost obstinate? Does it exhibit chameleon-like qualities—regularly changing its shape depending on when the definition occurs or who is doing it? Is it not only new but also one-of-a kind? When undertaken by teams, such perplexing problems out of a mixture of respect and precision are often given favorite and affectionate playful classifying names such as the artful dodger, tricky Dick or the extra-terrestrial.

2. Processability. Is it solvable through a dry run of conventional processes? Are the results sufficiently complete and persuasive to argue that the current state of the art or best practices are adequate and sufficient to assure mastery? Is the solution complete and holistic? Is all taken care of? But suppose it resists? Behaves like a square peg in a round hole? Or somehow can only be squeezed through and many parts are left over? Or seems finally in excess of all basic measuring and managing modes, speaks a foreign language, looms large and is too important and worrisome to ignore, acquiring in this case mythological stature: a fierce composite of Proteus and Prometheus—over-reaching technology and endless flux?

3. Data Base. Does the problem exceed or fall within the range of existing data banks and defining and processing metrics? Are the problem and its variations accommodated by and accounted for by what descriptors already exist? If not, then that immediately signals not only the emergence of a different kind of problem, but also one that involves a data quest. But what kind of data? Does anyone have it? How

much? Will it ever be enough? Finally, did we suddenly and unknowingly cross over the threshold into epistemology? When a problem exceeds what we currently known, and when it also exhibits difficulties of definition and processing, then in effect it describes the parameters not only of innovation, but also of its own companion data research agenda. It is now not just stubborn but a total outsider behaving like an intergalactic time and space traveler or probe.

Although triage generally works, it is not infallible. Mislabeling may occur. If it walks like a duck it must be a duck. The tip is familiar but its hidden depth may not be. The impulse generally is to be risk-adverse—to classify and process every problem so that one size fits all.

But there are telltale signs that give pause and compel a return to the drawing board. A number of parts are left out. Precious containers behave like sieves. The debris of processing machines that are overwhelmed litter the floor. Now there is no question that it is broken and needs to be fixed. Above all, that most nagging question of all, "Yes, but . . ." is encouraged and granted new creative value and focus. In this case, the emperor without clothes becomes a naked problem without a solution.

In summary, then, what has been gained? Basic operations have been affirmed and can continue. Tried and tested rituals can proceed to process now tried and tested problems. The workforce generally has a clearer idea of what innovation is by what it uniquely has to engage and solve. It also has an anticipatory understanding of the accountability of solutions criteria and conditions. The organization discovers it has a data research agenda. And finally, problem profiling and triage have created a fascinating group of somewhat unclassifiable problems, all of which stand at the threshold of the company's future, awaiting their being welcomed as its cutting-edge messengers of innovation.

Chapter Eight

Innovation Prep

CEO Conversations

Preparing the way for anything new or difficult is a neglected art. It requires anticipatory reflection and creative thresholds instead of direct and impatient assault. For example, the senior management of a small high-tech firm made an executive decision to promote companywide innovation. That was summarily announced as not only a crash course but also a crusade. Everyone in the organization would be involved. A designated steering group was appointed. Tangible results were to emerge within six months. Breakthroughs would be rewarded with one-time bonuses.

Does all of the above sound disturbingly familiar? Does any of it cause you to squirm and groan? Or do you find nothing wrong? In any event, by the time six months came around the company had nothing to show for its efforts. As a consequence, three of its vice presidents (marketing, human resources, and strategic planning) were dismissed. Then, troubled and confused, the CEO decided to call in a consultant with the idea of a quick fix and cleaning up the debris. I was that consultant.

Our first meeting started off with the CEO venting for ten minutes. My reaction was to listen and to wait patiently and then afterward to slow everything down and try to engage him in a general if not almost philosophical discussion of innovation. "Innovation is one of the most difficult objectives to accomplish. It is never easy to introduce. Its definition is slippery. Many argue as to what innovative really is and what it isn't. And whether everyone is creative."

Then I moved on to specifics. "How many of your managers in your judgment exhibit innovation? What percentage of the workforce do you estimate are creative? Do you believe employees can be trained to be creative or is such ability basically innate?" We also talked about innovations that oc-curred in the past in the company, as well as in the industry. "What were they? Who brought them forth?"

My strategy was to suggest that innovation is complex and not in the same league as announcing a salary increase or benefit package. In short, my goal was to encourage a more reflective and deliberative approach. I tried to give the impression that we both had all the time of the world to sort this thing out.

The approach worked. In closing the session, I suggested another one the next day to go over what apparently hadn't work and why that was the case. The CEO responded: "Let's make it early in the day before things get clut-tered and my time is gobbled up."

I found the CEO the next morning, not anxious to have another philo-sophical discussion but instead to get down to cases. His game plan clearly was to come up with a new and this time successful launching process for innovation in the company. I was reluctant to totally abandon the process of dialogue or lose what had been captured the day before. But the CEO was hot to trot, so I tried to weave together all three elements of reflection, evalua-tion, and action—what I viewed as the essential trinity for preparing the way for all new initiatives.

"OK," I said, "But first let's look at how we launched this initiative in the first place. That immediately puzzled the CEO: "Why should an announce-ment even be an issue for reflection, evaluation, and action?"

"We could get into an extensive discussion of how you announce deci-sions in general," I responded. "But I know you are anxious to get to the heart of this particular situation. So let me just ask whether there is anything special about innovation—the way we talked about it yesterday—that might affect the way the announcement was made?"

The CEO, musing out loud, recalled "Many are uneasy about innovation, many feel they are not creative. And I would even say that many may not know what innovation is, or be fully aware of what it could mean to the future of this company."

"Exactly! Given all these apparently legitimate concerns and hidden ques-tions," I asked, "What, in retrospect, would you have done differently about announcing the initiative?"

"With the benefit of hindsight, I guess, I would have used examples. Big ones, and many little ones, as many I could think of; some of those we talked about yesterday. I might have told them the story of what was done at 3M You know that article you gave me on their fifteen-minute system. Above all, I would try to strike a balance: While I don't want innovation to appear facile or accidental, I also don't want it to appear distant and impossible, beyond their reach, reserved for only R&D types."

"Good! So now we know that we can't just drop an announcement like a bomb without taking the chance that it will blow up in our face. OK, so that was not the best way to start and you already have found another way. It is interesting that you mentioned R&D. A little sidebar if I might?"

The CEO nodded and leaned forward. I continued, "Thomas Edison still holds the record for more patents than anyone else to this day. Of course, he may have been an inventing genius, but he had others working with him who were not Edisons. So he developed for himself and all his employees idea quotas. But he also knew that some ideas were big and many would be small; so, for example, he gave himself six months to come up with one new major idea, and a number of smaller ones. I mention Edison because he may be telling us something. His emphasis was not on inventions but ideas. Maybe that holds a key for the company and innovation. Maybe the process we want to get going is IG—Idea Generation. And maybe what we have to do is to encourage each employee to work on his ID—his own Idea/Innovation Diary—which is private and not available to anyone unless he says it is."

The CEO nodded reflectively. "You're right. The focus is really on ideas. We can't all be Edisons and match his record, but if we can get our people to write down what they think and what they have come up with we will be way ahead of the game. In fact, I never told anyone this, but I keep an idea journal by my bedside. OK, let's keep going. This is good stuff."

"OK let's go on to the next point. The initiative was presented as a crash course and a crusade. Put yourself in your employees' place. How would you have reacted to such a statement?"

The CEO snapped, "I would have resented it. I don't like being stampeded into anything. And I personally I don't warm to the cheerleader role. Worst of all, it sets us up for success or failure. We either make it or we fold. Besides, nothing could be further from the truth. We are actually doing quite well and all indications are that we will have solid sales for the next three to five years. So this was a future-oriented activity. But, OK, I see where you are going. What you are saying is that we should have just told it like it really is—as way of getting a leg up, insuring our future success. Right?"

"Absolutely," I quickly answered. "And maybe even to grow another business or at least another division. When the juices start to flow, you never finally know what people will come up. Now, pressing on, why a timetable of six months?"

The CEO bristled, "Now I think that was perfectly defensible. You can't have an open-ended arrangement without limits and without closure. I would let that stand."

"OK," I said and then paused, "But suppose nothing happens within six months? Do you shut everything down or let it just go on? Or suppose then something surfaces by month seven, something else by month eight. What then? How will that six month deadline look?"

The CEO interrupted: "Maybe arbitrary, even dumb .But there has to be some oversight and control. They have to know that they will be held accountable."

I mildly protested, "But accountable for what? You did not put a dime into this. You are not providing any training. You are not giving people time off. You are not sending them to any conferences. You are not even buying them books and magazines to read. You put this pot of money aside for bonuses but if no one comes up with anything, even that money won't be spent. I understand every executive's need for control and outcomes, but deadlines and innovation are not compatible, unless you are willing to settle for half-baked goods prematurely delivered before their time."

The CEO was quiet. Had I pushed too hard? I stepped back and took another tack, "Instead of control, you may want to go for indirect monitoring. Schedule weekly brown bags or pizza lunches (you pay). Mix divisions, levels, shifts. Have the supervisors just listen; tell them not to talk, just take notes. Carry forward those notes to the next level then to the next and then to senior management. Walk around, drop in on sessions unexpectedly, listen for a change."

The CEO sighed, "Well, it makes sense not to dictate creativity. It's like pushing spaghetti. It just won't behave the way you want it to. Well I guess you're also questioning my picking an innovation steering group. Did I do anything right?"

I said reassuringly, "You came up with idea of an innovation initiative, and that is right as rain. But I am curious. What was your thinking here? What did you hope to accomplish with this steering committee?"

The CEO sat back and thought: "Well, we picked people from each division. Each had an excellent record and had given some evidence of being creative. The idea was they would model for each of their divisions the behaviors to produce results."

I agreed "That makes a lot of sense. Modeling is critical. That is what Edison did. But here's my problem. It either has to be companywide or not. It is either going to be collective or not. Innovation often occurs with the least likely people and in the least likely ways. Besides, most selected steering groups are political. Those chosen are always the same ones picked. The winners of trips to Hawaii are always the ones who win again and again. Good for the few winners, lousy for all the rest who may get used to being losers; and there are always more of them than winners. Besides, everyone in the division will rib their representative to death and make him regret they ever were chosen in the first place. Finally it will be seen as a transparent way again of maintaining control. Make it egalitarian. Inclusive not exclusive. Fish or cut bait."

The CEO protested, "OK, OK, but what's wrong with incentives? It's been used since the beginning of time and it works."

I conceded, "You're right. Generally it works. It certainly has been effective for years in sales especially. But money and innovation have nothing to do with each other. It is a mismatch. Incentives stimulate only the familiar not the different. Besides, such incentive-driven innovations will generate a lot of look-alikes of what you already have. But you will not get anything different."

The CEO was not ready to toss in the towel, "Well, what should we do? Drop the idea of incentives altogether?"

I again became reflective, "I am not sure. My instinct tells me that it is a question the employee should tackle. See what they come up with. Make it part of the creative challenge. I have to confess. I am a little old-fashioned. To me the best incentive is the future of the company—the future of my job. Or as one worker put it to the COO: 'Your job is to keep this company around so that I can collect my pension.'"

The CEO leaned forward, "I agree. I am old fashioned that way too. And that worker is right. You can't have growth and change unless you are around to try both. But it's the executive's job to look ahead and to decide now what will keep us around later."

He stood up and held out his hand, "Well, I think our exchange has set us on a new course. I now see why care must be taken with certain initiatives—preparing the way as you call it—thinking it through. I would like you to stay with us on this project, through all the stages for as long as it takes."

"Be happy to do so."

"And let's get together soon and hold another seminar, OK Professor?"

POSTSCRIPT

I nodded smiling and said to myself, "He was right on both counts. I am a professor and it was a seminar." But after I left and was walking down the hall, I realized that he was a professor as well, and that good seminars are always shared if they are to be seminal.

In any case, in less than three months three major employee-generated proposals for innovation passed the review committee and were on their way to implementation. Many others followed. All were energized by the Idea/Innovation Diary, which often led to small nondramatic changes that could not be called innovative but just different ways of doing things. Above all, the employees were entrusted with the future of their jobs and the company rose to the challenge and became preeminent and permanent idea generators.

In the process what were the lessons learned? Innovation should never just be announced. Preparation is required. Examples should be given from the company itself, from the industry. Innovation should not appear facile or fortuitous but also never beyond reach of the rank and file. Speed is not relevant. Deadlines are the enemy of creativity. If you have to have quotas, stress number of ideas. Urge all to develop an Idea/Innovation Diary. Deadlines and innovation are not good partners. Keep everything open ended like the process itself. But stir the pot. Schedule weekly brown bags. Top management should not pick innovation teams. The effort is collective or it is not. Besides, it is not a political popularity contest. Money and innovation have nothing to do with each other. It is a crass mismatch and will not stimulate difference but incremental familiarity. If you need an incentive systems, let it be employee designed. It is likely to be creative in its own right.

The ultimate preconditions for innovation are environmental. The key variables are identified and summarized below:

Situation	From	To
1. Culture	Directive	Questioning
2. Focus	Same	Different
3. Structure	Closed	Open
4. Systems	Mechanical	Biological
5. Information	Limited	Shared
6. Distribution	Insiders	Network
7. Communication	Vertical	Horizontal
8. Status	Official	Unofficial
9. Incentives	Financial	Environmental
10. Quality	Prescribed	Evolving

Chapter Nine

Innovation Advocates, Enthusiasts, and Evangelists

The new and the young resemble each other: both are heady, assertive, and arrogant. Both seek to be free of origins and history, to exist independently, on their own, without any debts or obligations to continuity. Enormously powerful, innovation can end old businesses, create new ones, impart new life to current ones—any or all of the above at any or all times.

The old dilemma of how to stir such creative upstarts is thus compounded by the fear that it will be an ingrate and bite the hand that feeds it. Innovative outcomes are thus always a mix of new starts and endgames. But acknowledging and managing such ambiguity, is not a familiar operating assumption of traditional leadership.

Who, then, are the principal supporters of innovation? And equally as important, why? There are minimally three kinds of leaders, and they differ and vary in degree of intensity.

The first are the CEO Advocates of the New. They know what innovation can do for their bottom line, morale, and organizational unity. Innovation is almost an addiction, a fix that they need to keep going and to preserve corporate identity. It is the critical means to all survival and growth ends. No purists, these leaders accept every version they can get.

They particularly encourage all incremental advances: variations of ingredients or amounts in familiar formulas, tweaks that reduce costs, short cuts that involve less time, packaging arrangements that grant another look. Of course they would welcome the genuinely creative and disruptive, which creates new markets and brands. But they view such developments as an ideal that is hard to rely on and come by. Better thus to settle for what is at a lower level, less radical, and easier to generate. In short, to these leaders, innovation is really marketing and advertising. All real creativity is invested in packaging and selling the New.

Second are the Enthusiasts. As CEOs they typically traffic in visions. They invoke the glories of what once was as benchmarks of what can be again. Often cheerleaders, they call upon all to rise to the new occasion of saving the company by regaining its previous leadership position and regain market share.

But other than passion and slogans they are not so much genuine leaders as, again, users of innovation. They know its power to lift and inspire, to stir the juices, and to promise salvation. They also know its carrying capacity to weather storms and to get through hard times. Their visions are thus more political and tactical but do not possess or speak from a knowledgeable core of creativity.

Typically they surround themselves with "me-tooers." Like the CEO, they have run out of growth options and reluctantly been backed into the creativity corner. They are neither comfortable nor happy being there; they do not number innovative types among their friends or associates and confess almost proudly that they do not have a creative bone in their body.

If they are members of the executive team, they believe they have to support the CEO. They generally do not submit any minority reports. Alignment so absolute and demanding that they are all obedient echoes. Whatever differences they may have are subdued by the triumph of chain-of-command protocol. In any case, unity rules, and innovation, for better or worse, is the unifier. The current situation is so desperate that it requires putting all our eggs in the creativity basket and searching for the magic bullet.

Finally, there are the true believers, the Evangelists. These leaders are authentic. They have been creative in their own right, understand the reluctance and hang-ups of artistic temperaments, and are aware of how difficult it is to coax and manage emerging innovators. Above all, they value what the creation of an innovative culture can do for a company over and above whatever it may create.

They understand its power to attract and keep talent, what it means to work in an environment that is alive and constantly curious, and to work with associates who are restless energizers. But above all, these leaders have some idea of how to make that culture happen—even more important, of what it is linked to.

Minimally, innovation is sustained by five factors:

1. It is linked to a vision of the Big New Idea. Indeed, by inhabiting the same ground as the CEO, creativity minimally and persuasively reinforces the focus on vision.

2. It is systemic. Innovation can lead the charge because it is macro-worthy—it inhabits the Pantheon.
3. It crosses the line—into the future. It thus invites the journey of unity of common commitment and thereby the potential of serving as an inclusive company culture.
4. Innovation is ideological. It is the epitome of transformation. As such, it is emblematic of change for all.
5. Finally, it supports a new kind of leadership that argues for a new partnership between the incremental and the disruptive and introduces such doubleness as a 21twenty-first-century training norm.

A double argument thus emerges: to identify the forces that traditionally and recurrently shape and reshape vision, on the one hand, and then to introduce and position innovation as the central driver of this brave new worldview on the other. Thus from the outset the beginnings and ends of creativity have to be linked to the same ambiguous interplay of such similar agents of vision.

In addition, innovation and vision so paired cannot be ordered or commanded to emerge. They have to be coached, even teased out. Their commonality indeed should come as a surprise. In short, it is the outcome not of action but of reflection—of stepping back, pausing, and taking in the whole—and then visioning the forces of origins and ends.

Such shaping of a new big picture thus should not be a deliverable already predigested or predetermined but an exploration of what is seminal and recurrent. Trainers thus have to develop exploratory models of vision and innovation. The initial one would be led by and for the executive team. Then it would be adapted for general workforce application. A special adaptation would then become the orientation program for new hires.

THE CONTENT OF VISION

What would be the content? Although the essentials of vision vary, the basic components always possess the recurrent and classic nature and behaviors of archetypes. The following five, it can be argued, have both the resiliency and pliability to be constant yet redefinable, and to sustain the illustrative examples that accompany each one: the new idea, systems, foresight, ideology and leadership.

1. The New Idea!

Ideas are still civilization's most powerful mind-altering drug. Whether used as a lens to see the world in a new light or as an instance of discovery and insight—"I have an idea!"—big ideas not only shape the big picture but also

contain embryonically its yet-to-be discovered versions. Conceptual nominations can range from the new globalism in which the world is of a piece
economically and ecologically or that it is now a flat and endlessly proliferating network, or both.

But in all instances the test is the power of reconception to see doubly—to
bridge the then with the now, and the now with the future. By seeking to
close if not eliminate the gap between continuity and change, ideas function
as the eternal version of the work in progress.

2. Systems

Systems are secrets connected by purpose. Although their patterns of meaning and relationship typically may operate beneath the surface even at great
depth, when discovered, displayed and tracked they prove to be startlingly
verifiable and unifying.

The focus of archetypal system inquiry is thus always twofold. First, can
all that is emerging fit in and be absorbed by existing paradigms? Or can
such organizing systems be revised or redefined to facilitate accommodation?

Failing that, are there new systems or ecologies that have the maternal
inclusiveness to accept and mother a new brood of those who do not look
alike and are contentiously independent? But lest the nominating process be
indulgent, all new or redefined archetypes must be systemic.

3. Foresight

Although looking ahead should be common to all archetypal inquiry, for
foresight to be genuine and brave it must abandon the predictability of extrapolation and systematically focus instead on the disruptive.

What's new must give way to what's next. In other words, strategic
planners not only have to become futurists, but also embrace both that pro-
fession's reading and techniques of the laws and behaviors of discontinuous
futures. Such anticipatory specialists over five decades have developed the
expertise to see the future as a transparent enigma worthy of archetypal
status.

4. Ideology

All forecasts are threefold. They identify the probable (most likely), the
possible (including wild cards) and the preferable (what is hoped for). It is
the last that offers the prospect or illusion of control and purpose, and that
always has constituted the ideology of archetypes.

The mediation between traditional and new values thus is potentially
directive and promises the exoneration of justification. But as with all re-

viewed and redefined archetypes, the outcomes must be totally inclusive, capable of diverse consensus, and futuristically sustainable.

In other words, ideology of all considerations invokes and applies its parallel partners to discipline its own quest. Otherwise ideology will render all aspiration as partisan and based on exclusivity. My keys to heaven should not lock you out.

5. Leadership

Who is in charge and who decisively chooses what future to pursue is critical. It must avoid at the outset the danger of archetypes becoming stereotypes. The future chosen must be imaged as itself innovative—incarnate so that they become one when fleshed or born.

Not unexpectedly that cutting edge exists at the periphery. The future that emerges is coincidental with upstarts and start-ups. Innovation emerges initially as a minority voice disturbing the universe.

The process of birth involves a number of transformations: imagining the unfamiliar; then imagining the unimaginable; then imagining the unimaginable as the familiar; then managing of the unmanageable. In the process, it has to structure the emergence of the future, but one that offers the comfort of at least a familiar alien from outer space.

A NEW EVANGELISM

Happily, a new version of CEO Evangelism has appeared, which is helpful in that it structures further the nature of leadership innovation intelligence. The new rallying cry from CEOs is "Make mistakes!" At least that is what Proctor & Gamble's CEO, A. G. Lafley, urged; and to make sure we got the message, he provided a table entitled "A. G. Lafley's 11 Biggest Innovation 'Failures.'" in his book *Game Changer* (2008).

Of course, the moment such errors are embraced, personalized and bear your name, wisdom and humility walk hand in hand. Actually, Lafley's advice is not new. Not too long ago, Richard Farson enshrined the same concept in more paradoxical terms: *The Success of Failure, the Failure of Success.*

Shortly thereafter Gary Hamel warned us about risk-averse CEOs and managers whose timidity may jeopardize both the current and the future bottom line. Finally another broadside was directed against complacent executives living off past capital by Gottfried and Schaubert in *The Breakthrough Imperative* (2008).

What is going on? Why this preoccupation with a conscious commitment to error? The conviction that failure is the absolute path to creative success? But is it . . . always . . . and infallibly?

And even if error is the threshold of creativity, how do we un-program a generation of overachievers and teach them how to stumble? And finally while we wait for this paradox to generate wonders, what do we do in the meantime? Hold our breaths and hope for the redemption of a failed innovation?

Hardly. Innovation leadership puts together a more sensible and imaginative set of initiatives to manage and stir the ongoing, the sudden breakthrough, and the way ahead. Here are at least three initiatives that leaders might launch in tandem that span the range of hedging bets and playing wild cards:

The Ongoing Mainstream—the Now

Failure aversion is not necessarily a bad thing, our innovative enthusiasts notwithstanding. Many of our most productive managers cannot handle or manage error. In a few cases it would drive them crazy. Nor should they have to.

In our craze for the eureka moment let us not overlook the strong and steady commitment to continuous improvement and the constant tweaking that generates incremental gains in products and services quality.

In other words, don't quit your day job. The business has to go on. It cannot be put on hold while the brain trust burns the midnight oil. Besides, you could not find a more exacting group to test the latest innovations than those who have successfully been working out the bugs and turning a sow's ear into a silk purse for many years. The mainstream still remains the ultimate reality check.

Tangential Breakthrough Teams—the Emerging

Search out those professionals with a high tolerance for paradox, ambiguity, and speculation—especially if they tend to be loners, a little ornery, and hard to get along with. Group them by their differences: disciplines, units, degrees, age, gender, nationality, etc.

Create as many teams as necessary, even if or especially if they overlap; ideally all should be impressed by themselves, think they are da Vinci's gift to the world, and miniaturize the whole. Suggest unfamiliar places where they can meet, but never during regular work hours or days.

Their agenda? Compile what is crazy. Make it clear it cannot be incremental or familiar. The ultimate test is that it must be a start-up—able to begin in a garage, spawn a completely new business, especially one that is life-threatening—one that if we don't create or adopt it, will put us out of business.

Nothing will be monitored or evaluated; no one will review the list. Every two weeks it is to be sent with any artifacts, drawings, or miniatures to the CEO and one other of your choice.

The CEO Seminar on the Future of the Future—the Innovative

While all this is going on, the executive team has to pull its collective head out of operations and become stargazers. Every two weeks they are to play leapfrog—while we are catching up let us also get ahead of the pack.

Nothing is out of bounds. The range of the meetings should be 360, the scope global, the topic or approach somewhat radical. Invite wild cards, an occasional end-of-world type, gurus on innovations, and even a few far-out pontificating academics.

The unifying subject is what's new but fused with what's ahead—it should have the durability of a mega-trend. The test of discontinuity is that every vice president should leave with a different scenario of creation in his head than what he or she came in with; and perhaps begins to have different dreams.

Will it all work? In a sense it has to. It spans the now, the emerging, and the brand new; it differentiates between the everyday doers, the off-the-wall creative types, and the big picture and policy-making chiefs at the helm.

Will innovation occur? Undoubtedly. The only questions are: How long will it take for the loners to collaborate creatively? What increases in innovation productivity will occur over time? And finally, how fast can the mainstream wire the new in place so as to become industry leaders?

Meanwhile, the stargazers will continue to prepare the agenda for the next decade while those celebrating failure have made an enemy of the future.

Part IV

Innovation and Integration

Chapter Ten

Innovation Range

Three Professionals and Their Process Preferences

The need for innovation is obvious; how to do it is not. To begin with, the subject is still beset by the perennial question of whether it should be across the board or limited to select types. Then too, there is the question of the role of company culture and the extent to which its support of innovation is sufficient to determine happy outcomes.

What direction should training take? Generic or customized? Can innovation potential even be measured let alone isolated in initial interviews? Lastly, what shapes creative company cultures? Above all, with innovation should not answers always emanate from a focus not on external products but rather internal process—on who embraces its pursuit, how it evolves, and what the contributions of company culture are to its emergence?

The task is not an easy one largely because it involves acknowledging an underlying dynamic that generally exceeds HR concepts and data. Thus, typically, professionals are defined primarily by what they possess not by what they favor—in this case, by the problems and processes they characteristically or compulsively choose. But preference also often generates repetition and reputation. A number of professionals are singled out as the in-house go-to expert or guru for certain kinds of problems. Others by their special past experiences, assignments or networks. A few by their knowledge of research sources.

But whatever their original education, training or specialty, the one developed and mastered trumps all. It becomes their signature—their individual best practice. And the preferences chosen in effect define their mission, sometimes their passion.

Of course such branding does not just happen. It evolves gradually, over time, often accompanied by false starts or inadequate outcomes—in short, specialization and its performance distinction are ruled imperfectly by success as well as trial and error. But what finally imparts special shape and direction is the purposeful interrelationship that exists between professionals, problems, and processes.

Moreover, that dynamic when describable may generate not only answers to the above questions but also a model of innovation behaviors to follow. A number of obstacles stand in the way, however, not the least of which is the expectation of uniformity—of one size fits all.

Not all professionals are innovative. Not all problems require creativity. And not all processes facilitate innovation. Indeed, professionals are defined by the problems and the means they choose to employ. To be sure, that choice often is dictated or influenced by the discipline of each professional, and by the culture of their education, training, and work experience.

But such determiners do not alter diversity. Difficult though it may be for some to admit, not all Ivy League MBAs are innovative. In short, the key across-the-board discrimination required is to designate which configuration of professional, problem, and process relationships optimizes innovation and which ones do not.

Such discriminations require profiling. In this case, problem profiling or problem triage. The extremes are quickly defined: run-of-the-mill problems and exceptions to the rule. Those in between are held aside to be subsequently sorted out and assigned to one of the original two. The deciding factor is whether the problem is processable by standard in-house procedures.

If so, then although it may be designated as a somewhat more complex variation on a theme, it is still finally dispatched to the standard musical category. Or if it is not, then it may be left in limbo for a while, later revisited, or finally although reluctantly designated as an enigma.

But the triage process though critical is not infallible or unbiased. Mistakes are made and underestimates regularly occur. Indeed, over time they acquire and reflect a pattern. Namely, many companies and professionals are risk averse. Although that may take many forms, in this context it leads to designating problems as ordinary when they are uniquely daunting.

Typically, problems are not given their just due because of inadequacy—it exceeds our calipers—or hierarchy—it is regarded as too small, inconsequential, or irrelevant to the mainstream of what typically is confronted. Strangely, such devaluation or trivializing is often covered up by bravado—by proudly proclaiming that we are equal and a match for whatever is thrown at us; or with the reassuring estimate that the bulk or nearly all of that which has been successfully solved before leaves little or nothing left over to trouble us.

But the truth is otherwise: problems typically sort themselves out following Pareto's famous 80-20 rule. The bulk are garden variety, familiar, and recurrent. They are feel-good challenges that routinely fold over and give up their solution without a fight. Not so the more exotic in-your-face disturbers of the peace that won't go away or be easily pacified. They stick in your craw and lead to sleepless nights.

These one-of-a-kind challenges are not just new; they are differently new. They even may bear the face and force of paradigm shift and such adjustment of perception may alter the percentage allocation and the degree of difficulty.

In addition, because of current pressures of competition and loss of market share, some companies driven to the wall may claim that the innovation ante is now upped to 30 or even 50 percent of the whole—that such a business tsunami results in a call to rally not just for a select few but all the troops to respond to the call for life-saving innovation.

But less panic and more precision is needed to save the day. Specifically, the key corrective and diagnostic required still remains the dynamic relationship between professionals, problems, and processes, as well as how problem definition and solution options are driven by professional preferences and the favored choices of company cultures.

At the heart of that relationship and what finally defines its yield is professional choice. Not inappropriately, triage may also serve to identify the following three basic types of professionals and their respective ideologies.

THE APPLIER: THE CONTINUITY OF RECURRENCY

Let us call him Mike. Companies could find no more exemplary embodiment of competency than this kind of problem solver and manager of problem-solving teams. Vigorous and rigorous, Mike is a supreme advocate of the capacity of a dedicated and disciplined workforce to be equal to any and all tasks.

But he is also aware of the need to constantly update and upgrade and thus not only regularly endorses training, but also suggests its content. To be sure, he finds it difficult to manage when layoffs occur and when such thinning out brings about basic gaps in skill sets.

A hiring freeze and the limits of training to offset such deficiencies jeopardize the importance of competency and continuity. But most troubling is the loss or erosion of the culture of company loyalty. Its persistence and pervasiveness may make the prospect of retirement attractive.

Mike, like Ecclesiastes, operates under the assumption that there is nothing new under the sun and that the way we have customarily processed change and challenge is sufficient. In fact, he would claim that success occurs in more than 90 percent of cases.

And when or if it fails to work, the fault lies not in the process but in its application. His repeated call is to go back to square one and to apply due diligence. He is vigilant about detecting short cuts or relying on dirty data. Indeed, when it still may not work even with all the correctives factored in, then he concludes that we don't know enough—that we need more data— even though we may reach the point where we never have enough.

Sadly this stalwart of standards is the enemy of innovation. He regularly affirms the status quo of problem identification, processing, and solving and asserts at every meeting that all we need to do is to return to basics and core competencies. As a professional his preferences are for problems that are familiar and of a piece—and that are aligned and in synch with the tried and tested processes that have been the source of success.

Indeed, success turns out to be his supreme obstacle. A long record and history of spectacular achievement is trotted out to clinch his case. But seldom or never are such best practices found by Mike to be ironically imprisoning and paralyzing. When the Mikes are among the retiring baby boomers, although we typically may lament their departure and the loss of institutional memory or know-how, from the point of view of innovation it may be a necessary cleaning of the house essential to embracing a creative kind of problem solving. The generation liberated from Egypt did not enter the Promised Land.

THE ADAPTER—THE CUTTING EDGE OF CONSTANT CURRENCY

Let's call this one Sheila. Like Mike, Sheila values constancy except in her case it is that of constant change. If Mike leans too heavily on the past, Sheila is embedded completely in the present. In fact, she regards the new as the now of the future.

No one can match her busy and often dizzying gathering and cataloging of cutting-edge best practices. Totally on top of her game, she is a tireless researcher of industry patterns and those of her professional counterparts. A voracious reader of the latest books and articles and a tireless attendee at conferences, she endlessly drops off Xerox copies of handouts in mail boxes with the intimidating note," Here's what's coming down the pike." Or particularly after an intensely stimulating conference she will send e-mails identifying lists of dozens of sources and links that require immediate follow-up.

Sheila epitomizes the Internet and blogging. She outgoogles Google. Her drive is to find the best that is, adapt it to fit, scale it so that it is absorbable, and present it on a platter as a customized deliverable. No small or mean feat because that involves a savvy knowledge of organizational structure and company implementation routes.

What she offers is a kind of package deal not accompanied by any internal depth analysis or diagnostics except that justified by what others have found, what they are doing with success, and what therefore can accrue to us. The problems and problem-solving processes identified and endorsed are whatever are the current preoccupations of the industry and the latest business analysts. And when new solutions appear on the horizon, she is quick to offer the more current replacement backup. As savvy survivors, evolution is our mantra and adaptation our salvation.

Clearly the Sheilas are preferable to the Mikes. At least we are not driving forward while looking in the rearview mirror. To be sure, her total championing of the new is often oppressive and undifferentiated. She herself is not a researcher; nor does she call for such originality or require it of herself.

Her exclusive strategy is to run the company's s nightly news program and to be consoled by its regular presentation of reality. But such truth telling may embody a number of major shortcomings or trade-offs.

The external becomes not only a substitute for the internal, but also the inside is systematically emptied to the point where all that remains is an operating top of Sheilas and an adjunct force of order takers. Outsourcing becomes the ultimate model of total adaptation.

But imitation is not innovation. Although dizzying in number, choice is still determining; and choices driven by currency are typically short term, which may preclude later positioning. Above all, the quick and multiple fixes to insure immediate survival fall short of the unique survival power of discovery. Every genuine breakthrough also is always a new business, potentially a new lease on life for your company, or if ignored, taken up by others and put you out of business. Finally, excessive adaptation and absorption in the present may lure and seal you off from a future that in fact is the preserve of innovation alone.

THE INNOVATOR—PERMANENT TRANSITION

Rachel has not come to her present fascination and embrace of innovation overnight. Indeed, she has passed through being both a Mike and a Sheila and is thus better able not only to understand and value their contributions, but also to be aware of how formidable and deflective they can be. Above all, what has steadied her focus and singled her out is a series of constant questions beginning always with "Yes, but," progressing to "I am not so sure that is the answer," and finally wondering out loud whether "the emperor has no clothes."

The first and recurrent threshold of innovation is thus problem uncertainty. What confronts us is not so clear or resolvable as the Sheilas would have us believe. The issue is often not in focus but blurred at the edges. Its center is busy and shifting and eludes easy or rapid classification. Its current diagnosis seems glib and enjoys a momentum of agreement that may be deceptively persuasive.

So-called second opinions lose their value when they turn out to be largely and obediently confirmatory. What makes the case for Sheila makes the more reflective Rachel uneasy.

She begins to note that neither the problem statement nor the solution is total or inclusive; major parts are left out or over. Could it be, Rachel wonders, that what we see is not really what is—that it is not only the proverbial tip of the ice berg, but also something not typically found in these waters? Suddenly, Sheila's flashy fashioning gives way and has less hold as Rachel begins to ask of the problem whether its erratic behavior is characteristic of the playful antics of the artful dodger or of tricky Dick.

Occasionally, mythological nomenclature is invoked to grant it formidable reccurency. Does it behave in mercurial or chameleon-like fashion like Proteus, or is it an over-reacher like Prometheus? What ultimately persuades and attracts Rachel is that none of the standard processes are able to tame or classify the beast.

But even that first stage of qualifying the problem is not enough. Rachel has to determine whether investing the problem with sufficient intransigence justifies and nominates its being granted the centrality of innovation. Rachel wants to make sure at the outset that pursuing this problem is worth her time and focus—that although elusive, it is not a will-o'-the-wisp, that its tantalizing tip has some depth to it, that it ultimately will not be perceived as a transparent enigma.

The qualifying tests of the next stage take the various forms used often to test trends and typically are not applied by or to the Sheilas. Does the problem appear to possess durability or is it temporary? An awkward transition that will be replaced by the return of cyclical stability? Will its ability to last be accompanied by continued impact and discontinuity? And if it gives way, does it embryonically contain its successor? Is this transition to be followed by a return to equilibrium or by a new transition—and that, in turn, by another until transition, not stability, becomes the norm?

Curiously, granting an enigma the status of being recurrently aberrational clinches for Rachel its being dubbed finally an innovative problem requiring an innovative solution. It also now becomes Rachel's characteristic choice as the defining driver of her professional identity.

Although Rachel has still far to go on her journey to innovation with no guarantees of success, what overall conclusions, if any, can be drawn at this point? The first and perhaps most obvious is the importance of problem triage. The question of whether all should subsequently be offered innovation instruction should not obscure the need for such minimum across-the-board triage discrimination training. Equally as important is its application to organizational differentiation. Problem profiling sets up professional profiling. Each of the three has to be granted their place, given the sorting out of problem definitions.

But the dilemma that often occurs is that of exclusivity—where each one claims it alone possesses the keys to heaven and seeks to drum out or dominate the others. Giving problems their separate due is to be followed by allowing and affirming professionals to make and honor their various choices and apply their craft.

Mike and all the other adapters of the tried and the true need to be given their head and process 80 percent of what is going on. The company thus remains operationally sound and continues to generate income. The Sheilas and all the appliers are invaluable reminders that more is changing than remaining the same; and further, that the question of what the competition is doing needs now to include what the research shows. But an absolute commitment to currency serves at best as a threshold for innovation but stops short of embracing its disturbing discontinuity.

Rachel and other innovators not only choose and define one-of-a-kind problems, but they do so with yields that normalize aberration as well. Indeed, the overall effect of granting each group its value and function is that collectively they may increase minimally the visibility, importance, and difference of innovation and thereby compete to attract new recruits to their ranks. But perhaps the most unexpected outcome is the linkage of innovation and leadership.

Minimally, three leadership options surface. The first is the recognition that the proper overall orchestration of and coexistence of all professional types requires balance and balancing acts of leadership. But that does not preclude the leadership initiative of assigning company priority to innovation, serving as its advocate and running interference; and pressuring HR to redefine and find the best and the brightest as the most skeptical disturbers of the peace.

Finally, although since many leaders are not innovators themselves or at least not now or even recently, they can nevertheless harvest its many benefits. They can position their leadership and organization at the intersection of present and future. They thereby can hearken to the leadership messages that innovation as the messenger and transparent enigma of the future has to deliver about where we should be going and what smart choices we should be making.

Leaders who do not fully embrace innovation's future are more followers than leaders, and they lead companies to lose their lead. But Innovation Leaders live the future, which is the principal reason they are often not understood and not chosen to lead. One would wish stretch, not shock, and enlightenment, not desperation, to be the midwives, which is the way we and the future work.

Chapter Eleven

Training and Taming Trouble Makers

A few years ago I was hired as VP of HR and inherited a fascinating challenge. The organization sought my advice on how to deal with excessive creativity. That was a new one for me. Most companies complain of its lack. What was equally puzzling was the perception that this was a problem. To say the least, it was intriguing. Here is the background.

The company was a recent amalgam. It was three organizations put together by a venture capital group to fill both a traditional and e-business market niche. The business plan was solid; so was the market analysis. The CEO and senior staff were experienced and seemed equal to the task of integrating the three cultures. The employees, carry-overs and new, seemed impressive.

Most important of all, it was working. All operational goals were met in the first year. By the second, profitability was lower than expected because of some unexpected and substantial cost increases. Corrective action had to be taken to insure cash flow. The more innovative projects scheduled to be implemented in the third and fourth year, were put on hold.

The reaction by the professional staff was not just strong but almost mutinous. For the most part they were entrepreneurs and had functioned on and off as independent contractors. They were risk takers. They had been hired with the understanding of profit sharing. Each employee was vested upon being hired and assigned a designated percentage share of earnings over and above salary. Moreover, such bonuses were to be separately given by a nonprofit foundation and research institute for tax purposes.

In short, they saw their get-rich prospects decline and in some cases disappear. And they were furious. Their solution? Infusion of more capital to absorb any losses and maintain solvency. But do not change the growth plan.

Do not alter what brought them all here in the first place. Move aggressively forward.

Fearful of wholesale departures on the one hand and extensive counter-productivity on the other, a major consulting firm was brought in to address the problem and to ease the transitions deemed necessary. Their initial contract was for six months, but by the end of the first month they threw their hands up in despair.

The consultants found the employees brilliant but impossible to work with. They were all prima donnas. They were narcissistic, and seemed incapable of working together. Each one had an exalted view of his own genius and indispensability. Above all, they were all disturbers of the peace. They did not even stay within their own divisions but roamed and poached and pouted. Nothing was getting done. They challenged and baited each other endlessly like spoiled children. They would "yes but" you to exhaustion. Recommendation: fire the lot and replace them with more docile creative types.

When that recommendation leaked out, one mischievous group who called themselves "The Troublemakers" and who were clearly able to work together at least in protest, decided to put together a list of criteria HR should use for the new hires. Secretly circulated, it was put in the form of a Q&A quiz:

Questions Typical Docile Answers Creative Responses

Questions	Typical Docile Answers	Creative Responses
1. Things are right or wrong?	Yes	Yes, No ,and Maybe
2. Technology is good or bad?	Yes	Both but it is also never neutral
3. Teams are always smarter.	Yes	But when they blunder....look out
4. Info-sharing is good.	Of course.	But who owns the data?
5. Customer is always right.	Absolutely.	No, but that is the challenge.

To the above, the following postscript was added: "None of the present members of the non-solving and non-understanding consultant team brought in here to "solve" us would ever come up with these questions let alone the right answers."

When the consulting team learned about the quiz and the postscript, they renegotiated the last five months of their contract and left in a huff. Their parting comment was that they did not want to be associated with failure.

Although I had no special reputation for pulling rabbits out of a hat, I always had a fascination with and even weakness for creative types and how they function or fail to in corporate environments. In any case, the company was desperate.

The first document the vice president of HR reluctantly gave me was the quiz. I was enormously impressed and said so, which led him to worry whether I was going to be part of the problem or the solution. He concluded that I probably was just like them and would only inflame the situation. He was half-right; I was like them, but I was also mindful of my bill-ables. I quickly made a mental note to pocket that quiz and use it sometime in a workshop on creativity.

A whole avalanche of questions were unleashed: Were these problems holdovers from some of the original cultures and unresolved in the new amalgam? To what extent did bad times serve as a catalyst, bringing to the surface behaviors that previously were problematic? Why did they call themselves "troublemakers"?

My instinct told me that this self-selected title was no small matter. Troublemakers is such a strong, almost self-abusing term. Is that the role they saw themselves playing in the present situation? Or were they always that way? I had never encountered the term before in anything but a pejorative sense.

My first task was to profile what makes a troublemaker a troublemaker. You need to go into the enemy camp and listen and record what troublemakers typically have to say. Here is what I found:

Trouble makers have been that way all their lives.

They are round pegs forced into square holes.

They take a perverse pride in not fitting in.

They confess that they are pains in the neck.

They concede they are the original "Yes but" types. raised to an excruciating level.

They enjoy being gadflies (but they were ultimately loveable and valuable).

They admit to being destructive, constantly stalling groups or divisions from moving forward and accomplishing their tasks.

It was even worse than I thought. In addition to all the above, I found them to be mono-maniacs harping on the same thing over and over again. They make mountains out of mole hills. They are perfectionists. Nothing ever satisfies them. They seek endless revisions, reviews, and reengineering. They are exhausting.

But they did have value. They often have saved companies a great deal of embarrassment by pointing out that the emperor has no clothes. They always question assumptions. Their favorite phrase is "Where is it written that we have to do it this way?"

They routinely stall the start of any project on a regular basis by constantly asking seemingly endless questions: What does the current research show? What do we really know? And how do we know that?

They constantly challenge the problem-solving process because of its predictable search for a solution proximate to the problem, whereas it may be hiding far away from the source of the difficulty. They also are compulsively futuristic. They devour science fiction and often believe organizations would be better off run on principles of sci-fi. Unhearkened to, they would easily become whistle blowers and cheer every recall. They are annoyingly creative.

But although one may concede their occasional value, most colleagues and companies would wish them gone. Where? To a university where they could rightly and appropriately plague students or to a think tank where they could drive other troublemakers crazy.

Nevertheless, here was a rare opportunity—not just a few but a whole host of troublesome but nevertheless creative types. The starting point was unique. Instead of beginning with managers who were not innovative and getting them to embrace deviant thinking and creative dislocation, these people were already there. In other words, the task was to work backwards. Instead of trying to make them creative, the aim was to civilize them without extinguishing the creative spark.

Would it be possible to preserve the best but restrain the rest? Imagine being able to extract from the role of the solitary troublemaker enough of the troublemaking positive essentials but adjusted to being a team player.

Could those who are not troublemakers be trained to bring special value to organizations badly in need of assumptions analysis, restructuring, and innovation? The gains in thinking outside of the box could be considerable, especially if the exasperating downsides could be eliminated or reduced.

But I was getting ahead of myself. I told myself to stay focused with the issue of being able to strike a balance between contrariness and cooperation."

Many were skeptical; some were convinced it could not be done—or not without trade-offs at both ends that would jeopardize the worth of the outcome. Certainly, the task was formidable and the odds daunting. But the prospect perhaps becomes less intimidating if we employ self-coaching—if we see this as a stage of personal leadership development—as an opportunity for internal dialogue.

What unique creature was I trying to build? A collaborative troublemaker. A human oxymoron. In other words, the turn-around required civilizing rather than trying to get rid of them.

Toward that end, three different role models were pressed into service: the researcher, the consultant, and the trusted advisor. Each model brings something special and even urgent to the creation of a professional. The researcher is preeminently a problem poser and definer. The consultant is preeminently a problem solver, a challenger of basic assumptions, and an uncompromising advocate. The trusted advisor articulates the conscience of a corporation, its integrity, and its humanity.

But here everything had to start from a different point. Typically, employees involved in creativity training and learning are not malcontents. They are reasonably bright, open, and balanced. To be sure, they also are at a point where they may unknowingly be complacent or stuck. They may have stopped short of getting to the next plateau.

Such states of inertia typically will not respond to the standard training incremental fare. Instead, what they may need is a jump-start—something discontinuous, a leap forward, a break in the predictable pattern—to get their attention. Indeed, the outcomes being sought require changing the way we perceive, examine, and relate to things, people, and situations. For what the reformed troublemaker produced to possess pivotal value, it had to be corrective on the one hand and liberating on the other.

The goal was to produce a totally different working arrangement and community. That involved creating their own working environment, which was to be self-designed, self-maintained, and self-governing, with no one in charge.

Their basic obligations were to each other and to the project. They were totally inward facing. They were to ignore the rest of the company and its rules of behavior and dress, especially with regard to working hours and days and access to labs, offices, or studios. They wanted 24/7 access.

They were completely in charge. A huge program board was mounted on the east wall that monitored project progress. Prayers and meditation sessions could be scheduled any time or day of the week and would never be regarded as an interruption. A padded tantrum room was reserved outside the work area. But increasingly it was used as a retreat and meditative space. It was named the Buddha room.

Although the expectations of change were substantial, they were not unreachable. If the training was to take hold, those involved would not emerge as new or unrecognizable but rather recast. Above all, the exposure to the roles of researcher, consultant, and trusted advisor were not abstract but company and project specific. Each employee, in other words, was asked to apply the principles of each model to his own style and to real in-house problems.

Did the training work? Yes. And did it take and last? Yes. Did it in fact civilize the troublemakers? Beyond our wildest expectations. Why was it successful? I had my own explanations, but at the last workshop meeting, which unsurprisingly they took over, the now collaborative mavericks described what moved their transformations. Here is a sample:

"We were not told what to do or become. A finished product was not held up as a template. It was all in our hands. Good thing too. What we produced was brilliant."

"They were great models to contemplate. I never thought of myself as being a consultant and therefore an advocate. The trusted advisor role blew my mind. I imagined myself working with our CEO. Except now I would not so much be telling him what to do but drawing him out, hopefully leading him down a more humane path. But to do that I really had to practice self-restraint, because I already had all the right answers."

"I loved the prospect of being a consultant. I am a permanent student. I pride myself on being unfinished. I have the feeling I could give myself a PhD. But what stopped me in my tracks was methodology. I recognized that I would have to design my own way through to an answer. I had always left that to institutions, which is so totally unlike me."

"I was amazed by the variety and diversity. We all thought we were all unique. And happily that did not change. But we were sealed within ourselves. We never understood or appreciated the hot stuff of others. And in a couple of exercises in which we had to work together, wow, five of us left the earth."

"I was worried all the time that we would be tamed and come out dull. But we had a great lion tamer who let us roar and jump when we wanted to. After a while we even forgot we were in a cage."

"I have always been a pain in the neck, too smart and big for my britches. I found out I don't have to be a pain to be smart. All I have to be is a cooperative troublemaker. It hurt!"

All believed that they had created a new culture of collaborative disagreement for the company. They embraced the tough discipline of each role in a unique way, harmonized it with their difference, and internalized a new whole.

The problem-solving formats and confidential dialogue protocols they produced were all masterful, intriguing, and often uniquely useable. Above all, it was wonderful to observe them now as part of a questioning culture that is principled, purposeful, productive, and innovative. And also happily, routinely civil—occasionally. But they would never make peace with bosses.

Chapter Twelve

Innovation as Convergence

It is usual to treat Leonardo as a scientist and as a painter in separate studies. And no doubt the difficulties in following his mechanical and scientific investigations make this a prudent course. Nevertheless, it is not completely satisfactory, because in the end the history of art cannot be properly understood without some reference to the history of science. In both we are studying the symbols by which man affirms his mental scheme, and these symbols, be they pictorial or mathematical, a fable or a formula, will reflect the same changes. —Kenneth Clark.

Every major forecasting effort of the last twenty-five years always has exhibited an intellectual core. To the traditional history of ideas, forecasters have added the history of future ideas. The key task has always been to discover the major forces in the present driving future development. What appears to be emerging now is a resurgence of the pursuit of unified knowledge.

What is there about the current situation and the next two decades that is pressuring and presaging a preoccupation with the integration and unification of all knowledge? Who are some of the major figures and what are the shaping factors that individually and collectively help to determine whether the content generated has the conceptual power to function as a mega-trend?

Three representative areas of convergent thought will be examined. The first deals with the technology and theology of convergence, the second with the socioeconomic and political dimensions of "connexity," and the third with the "consilience" of science and the humanities. Finally, a summary of the range and substance of these three areas should serve to establish the basis for designating convergence as a mega-trend of the twenty-first century.

CONVERGENCE: TECHNOLOGY AND THEOLOGY

According to many, "the universe of one science" exists and presupposes a constellation of common research inquiries and activities. There is always the many before there is the one. Gradually, however, discrete and scattered strands of inquiry coalesce, become initially a cluster, then a consortium of cross-fertilization, and finally converge and emerge as a powerful force with a common theoretical and intellectual agenda.

To make sense of this dynamic progression and to provide reassuring tangibility, the future is often rendered as a new creation story or science fiction focused on the specifics of creating, for example, autonomous humans, amplified and potentially ageless. And so begins the sometimes uneasy partnership between technology and theology—two frontiers that already have been crossed. The first involves the "internal pharmacy," by which humans can be maintained at an individualized optimum level automatically.

A metabolic profile is developed for each individual, and to it are pegged all known medications, chemicals, and nutrient supplements to maintain optimum balance. When implanted, it monitors the various functions and vital signs that are to be maintained and dispenses the appropriate chemical in the appropriate amount to maintain efficacy.

All of this builds on new technology utilizing implants and sustained release of drugs or electrical charges, in treatment of specific diseases (cancer or diabetes). As a result there is already considerable expertise and even familiarity with the procedures.

But if this is a quantum jump, it is because it is based on a total understanding of the interacting and integrating dynamics of the entire human system. It is that convergence of knowledge that provides the intellectual base for producing a complete metabolic profile of each individual. Perhaps, its greatest value, given genetic predictors and family history, is to provide proactive options to be involved in preventive medicine.

The second convergence of this magnitude is what has been called "the third intelligence. Incremental knowledge only adds to the overload. What is needed is recognition of patterns and paths between and across knowledge areas. Only such models of integrated knowledge clusters can then comprehend the multiple reverberating effects of drug interactions, the dynamics of global pollution and recovery, and finally thinking in ten dimensions. But easier said than done: How do we get there?

Our technology needs to undergo a double development. First, it has to be given a range of sensory inputs (with enough blank space to accommodate more); second, it needs the ability to create its own perceptions. Development along cloning lines is not the way to go. That is the incremental direction. What we need is an interfacing chip that can understand the way we think and conceive and yet possesses its own intelligence, which is intentionally different and even divergent.

It is a permeable relationship—sometimes equal, sometimes not; sometimes one dominating, sometimes the other, sometimes neither. But although the fit initially at least has to be mutual and consensual, it must be allowed to develop, on the one hand, and on the other hand, to call on other means when the problem exceeds the combined power and comprehension of the third intelligence. In short, the projected convergence requires human-technological intervention in the evolution of the species—a new Adam and Eve—with the midwife being unlimited synthesis.

But is it doable? In the human brain there is no distinction between hardware and software. The biological neural networks of the brain are instead a special kind of intelligent hardware that is not completely fixed at birth but evolves and modifies with time as the person grows and learns. In other words, whereas our current intelligent machines are dualistic, the brain is already integrated—already hardware and software. The neural networks of the brain change with patterns of use and experience, and in the process they generate "the mind," which is a combined creation of the brain and information and learning.

Increasingly the brain and the mind develop a master-servant relationship. In other words, while it is no small matter to design "brain chips," it is an incredibly difficult task to design "mind chips." Finally, the brain-mind is a self-programming, self-teaching, and self-managing system. It is autonomous.

Reconfigurable hardware, once programmed for sufficient autonomy, has about it the promise of being self-regulating, thus supportive of precisely the way the mind thinks and learning proceeds. The test of its success as a mimic of the mind is whether it helps to develop information impact and causes change.

Sometimes, the applications and objects of projected convergences surface even before the theoretical and intellectual convergence knowledge base has fully solidified. One occurred after the Civil War and involved the convergence of the mechanics of a piano and firearms technology to produce the first rudimentary typewriter. The results of convergence are greater than the sum of its parts.

In the process, science increasingly will sound like religion. But that is not totally surprising. In fact, if nature were not so profound to begin with, science would not exist. There would be nothing to explain, no patterns to be found, no order to be discovered. The classic comment by Einstein is correct: "The most incomprehensible thing about the universe is that it is comprehensible."

Thus, science's quest for convergence is really and always a quest for the origins of all things. In this connection, the human genome is the mother lode. It offers re-creation. Much of the intellectual novelty and power of convergence is that it will finally bring about a fusion of science and religion, Prometheus and God.

Indeed, the scope of scientific inquiry was originally the exclusive preserve of priests and mystics. And although the issue of the origins of the laws of nature is strictly speaking not a scientific but a metaphysical question, that separation is no longer respected or valued.

But three major objections surface. First, what have been called patterns of coming together occur all the time in nature and just as often fall asunder. But to invest the occasional or even frequent patterns of convergence with the force of a complete and permanent arrangement is to inflate a partial occurrence with a significance that just is not there.

Second, humankind is not a singular entity. Evolution operates not by progress but by diversity and variation, and there are many varieties of *Homo sapiens*. Moreover, the complexity of the designs of human societies is greater than that of nature. The number of variables is so great that they cannot be understood, let alone managed. Finally, the convergence really seeks to attack the last great frontier and to take on time itself. It is nothing less than the ultimate presumption of immortality.

The last issue is a real one, but the proponents of convergence are not willing at this point to contemplate anything so absolute or arrogant. In effect they are really talking about longevity or relative immortality, not an absolute condition. But what is dramatically clear is that the new technology born of convergence is in effect a theology. Indeed, the ultimate synthesis may be to make them one.

Misgivings about understanding and managing human and societal complexity is in fact a central focus of Geoff Mulgan, who directs a think tank, teaches at University College London, and—most important for our focus—was a member of former prime minister Tony Blair's Policy Unit. The title of his book *Connexity* not only introduces a new and futuristic term to the discussion of synthesis, but also takes a new direction.

Mulgan's concern is with culture, especially the culture of politics, government, and social change. His contribution to and reinforcement of the theory of convergence is thus offered from a social science perspective. To Mulgan, human history basically has been preoccupied by three major definitions of the sociopolitical self. All three currently coexist in different countries, societies, and classes because the world is a total time machine.

The first one is the culture of dependence in which freedom is in very short supply and a single dominant and dominating ideology and theology is tyrannically in place. Deservedly, maintains Mulgan, wherever that kind of bondage prevails it is appropriately designated as the dark ages. Happily, declarations of independence, through both revolution and evolution, ushered in a culture not only of democratic, egalitarian, and proactive discourse but also of unbridled and unshackled inquiry. Indeed, it is from this emancipation that the twins of democracy and science emerged and flourished. But Mulgan finds substantial evidence for the emergence of a third or new phase: interdependence. Like the phases that preceded it, interdependence has come about as an antidote to excessive freedom and to the notion of the self as sovereign.

In conditions and cultures of freedom, the individual rules supreme and feels free to call upon all the means of his society to protect and even increase his freedom, especially when anything appears to challenge, contain, or abridge it. The net result is an ambiguously liberating and self-indulgent society of free-wheeling, self contained, autonomous individuals whose orbits are unrestrained and undirected. That is basically a win/lose process in which the self wins but social coherence loses.

But what Mulgan sees increasingly emerging are individuals and societies that increasingly accept that they are connected to everyone and everything exists in a web of mutual interdependence evolving toward a higher integration. The alternative culture increasingly accepted and encouraged by both psychologists and sociologists is one in which "the self is perceived as less of a given, less complete, less whole. . . . Maturing means accepting your incompleteness, your permeability to other people." Although Mulgan clearly favors this new image of the self in an increasingly interconnected society, he sees it as largely voluntary in Western cultures and more of a tradition in Eastern cultures. But he does argue rightly that it is being hastened on the one hand by need and by enlightenment on the other.

Thus, the incredible commitment in business to interdependent teams is being driven by intense competition and by the capacity of teams to be more innovative. Indeed, that "teamness" is celebrated by a new term—"Coopetition"—a fusion of cooperation and competition. Compelled or chosen, the limits of freedom are more than offset by the benefits of collaboration. The new ideal of the future is a reconstitution of identity, which will take the form of the collectivized individual who encloses self and other in the same person.

Mulgan further identifies three major laws of interconnectedness. The first is generally a corrective. The notion of technological advancement as discrediting what it ostensibly displaces is not borne out by patterns of evidence: Throughout the twentieth century physical mobility and communications grew in tandem rather than as substitutes.

Electronic culture did not replace books; sales have increased. In fact, both appear online in Amazon.com. The growth of video conferencing ironically boosted the market for hotel conference centers. Economists claimed that 80 percent of economic growth in the 1950s was accounted for by technological change, but studies have shown the primary role played by ideas and knowledge growth in driving economic growth.

Thus, connexity tends to be cumulative. Each new medium of communication does not replace its predecessors so much as complement them. Connexity rests on the recognition of recurrent coexistence—that is, how so-called opposites or disconnects are perceived as being in tandem—as cooperating. Even in science, which tends to regularly throw out the past and to be noncumulative, what is really discarded are the conclusions not the theories; the Greeks still haunt Darwin.

The second key law of increasing connectedness is the convergence of the world economy and world ecology. The environment has become the supreme advocate of interdependence and compelled a recognition of a single world, without borders and perceived as a single whole from outer space. The same recognition is attributed to the global economy, which is a composite of world trade, world direct investments, global diffusion of technologies, and an integrated communications system. Indeed, the info-sphere has the same integrated qualities of the biosphere.

In fact, Mulgan claims that we need new maps of the world to replace the standard ones of land masses delineated by political masters.

> Today the links matter as much as the territory, and our maps should show the volume of trade, of messages, or of movements of people. We need maps that can measure the ease of communication or travel in terms of how long it takes to send a message or to move a thing between two points—giving us a map of the world made up of isomorphic lines, rapidly coming closer together over time, until most parts of the world are within twenty-four hours of each other in physical movement, and a few microseconds in terms of the movement of information. (*Connexity*, p. 23)

The intense economics of exchange in a global economy has created world prices for goods and services, where in the past there were only local prices. In fact, that is precisely the source of intimate competition: a plant in Ohio is aware of the price and the quality of the same product made in Korea; and more seriously, so are its customers.

Homo sapiens is increasingly becoming also *Homo economicus*, a person who defines himself as a series of multiple exchanges, who functions in an interconnected world made up a of a lattice of contracts and reciprocal flows of goods and services. The effort conceptually to master such complexity brought about the reinvention of political economy, which ironically existed as a single discipline in the nineteenth century and then was split wrongly into political science and economics. As a result, we have political scientists who know nothing about economics and economists who know little about politics.

But unified again, the two disciplines have produced a significant body of research that affirms interconnectedness. Institutions of free trade have proven more effective than those designed to prevent or contain war, and more

diplomatic activity is now devoted to managing trade than to managing security. Global economy is thus as good an advocate of peace as the United
Nations, if not better. The UN is still a creation of barriers of sovereignty
rather than their removal by interconnectedness. Another agent of global
convergence is ecology. Pressure for ecological integration has become a
critical force that acknowledges and defines both.

Finally, Mulgan's third law of convergence or connexity provides those
like himself who are preoccupied with social, political, and economic design
with a model to image and to design a self-organizing society, as opposed to
one made up of separate self-organizing groups, the favorite isolated states of
politicos. The philosophical idea that best expresses this ideal of a self-
organizing society is self-creation. Rather than thinking of systems in rela-
tion to an external environment, we should see them as autonomous, circular,
self-referential, primarily concerned with their own organization and identity. The creation of a culture of autonomy suggests how a society might
organize itself, adapting and evolving without the need for hierarchies and
belief systems that stand above people enforcing continuity and responsibility. If each human life makes the transition from dependence through independence to interdependence, then societies can make the same transition,
evolving into a common framework within which each element can take
responsibility for itself and for the whole. To Mulgan, the promise of connexity is thus ultimately utopian.

Perhaps, the supreme spokesperson and articulator of the unification of all
knowledge is Edward O. Wilson. In fact, his book *Consilience* is subtitled
"The Unity of Knowledge." In this role, he follows the lead of many who
called the pursuit of the unity of all sciences, the Ionian Enchantment. The
roots go back at least to the sixth century BC and to Thales of Miletus, who,
according to Aristotle, was the founder of the physical sciences. Wilson also
acknowledges the pioneering work of Einstein, "the architect of grand unification in physics . . . Ionian to the core" (*Consilience*, p. 5).

But Wilson goes further in at least two respects. First, he takes as the
scope of future convergence nothing less than all knowledge—not just the
sciences but also the social sciences and the humanities: "Nothing fundamental separates the course of human history from the course of physical history"
(*Consilience*, p. 11). Second, he envisions a coincidence of vision: namely,
that the convergence of all knowledge will in effect be a creation story and
tell us once and for all who we are and why we are here, and thus it will test
and affirm perhaps Holy Writ, the science of mythology. It will in essence
constitute the twenty-first-century version of the struggle for the soul.

What is particularly instructive about Wilson's views is his identification
of what has or may continue to prevent or compromise convergence. Thus,
socially and politically we are typically unbalanced: "the vast majority of our
political leaders are trained exclusively in the social sciences and humanities,

and have little or no knowledge of the natural sciences" (*Consilience*, p. 14). And no one appears to be concerned about such a lopsided and fragmented situation. Nor is it often any better on the other side. There are physicists who do really not know what a gene is and biologists who are ignorant of string theory. The "fragmentation of expertise was further mirrored in the twentieth century by modernism in the arts, including architecture" (*Consilience*, p. 43). In short, pieces are being passed off routinely as wholes across the board.

Wilson offers a real-life illustration of typical fragmentation. Governments generally have a difficult time developing a policy to manage dwindling forest preserves of the world. Clearly, this is a multifaceted problem. Minimally, it involves ecology, ethics, economics, and biology. Picture a quadrant in which each of these four fields inhabits one-quarter of the quadrant.

The fact that four perspectives are identified in the first place is a major step forward, but it deteriorates rapidly from this point on. Immediately, arguments of jurisdiction or territoriality surface. That is rapidly followed by the ego of size and extent: how big or small each of the quadrants should be. In the process, mutual ignorance comes to the fore. Each field knows little or nothing about the others but enough to challenge pretensions to the throne and their being in the arena or quadrant in the first place.

Let's change the configuration a bit, suggests Wilson. Draw a series of concentric circles around the central intersection cutting across all of the sections of the quadrant. That establishes the agenda of consilience. The small innermost circle would be a set of minimum interfaces that would permit each discipline at least to acknowledge both its contributions and limitations. The larger, more inclusive circles stress connections rather than separations. The largest circle offers the collective, cumulative, and convergent. The higher one goes in the food chain, the bigger the bite.

But there are few established ethical guidelines and those that exist generally are not shaped by ecological knowledge. The economics of sustainable yields is still a primitive art. What biologists know derives from short-term observations. Ecologists have been embarrassed by the boomerang of their premature death announcements, as nature and animals often have bounced back.

So there is a double problem: each discipline needs to deepen its own knowledge; and each discipline needs to know more about what it has in common with the others. Consilience compels the highest, most encompassing and inclusive concentric circle, which provides the optimum number of crossing and bridging points across boundaries.

It is Wilson's contention that when a convergence agenda becomes paramount then increasingly the likelihood is that concentric circles rather than quadrants will be the primary structure. But the agenda needs to be shaped by the leaders of each discipline in order to guide the research throughout the entire enterprise. The politics of positioning may be necessary for the interfacing benefits to be realized in daily exchange. There are, at least to Wilson, four great chasms that need to be bridged. They are the conflict between the cultures of science and the humanities; the nature/nurture controversy; the physiology and psychology of the brain/mind; and the racial superiority/ inferiority of world cultures.

Not much progress has been made because each side believes it is right and the other is wrong. According to Wilson they are both right. Indeed, the most difficult conflicts to solve are not between right and wrong, but a conflict of rights. Significantly, the way that Wilson seeks to bring about a more cooperative attitude and ultimately consensual convergence is in fact to reframe the opposition in terms that bring all the conflicts together under one roof.

For example, the conflict between the two cultures is less the result of a fundamental antagonism than the creation of artificial territorial lines. If that were replaced by a "broad and mostly unexplored terrain awaiting cooperative entry from both sides" (*Consilience*, p. 137), a larger, more formidable but more reconcilable version of the conflict would emerge.

All human behavior and its artifacts are transmitted by culture. Biology has a share in the creation and transmission of culture: "The question remaining is how biology and culture interact, and in particular how they interact across all societies to create the commonalties of human nature. What, in final analysis, joins the deep, mostly genetic history of the species as a whole to the more recent cultural histories of its far-flung societies" (*Consilience*, p. 137)? Although Wilson admits that at the present time no one has the total solution, the answer already is apparent: "From diverse vantage points in biology, psychology, and anthropology, they have conceived a process called *gene-culture coevolution*. In esens , the conception observes, first, that to genetic evolution the human lineage has added the parallel track of culture evolution, and, second, that the two forms of evolution are linked" (*Consilience*, p. 138).

Similarly, the great divides between different human societies have nothing to do with race, religion, or the innate superiority or inferiority of certain peoples. It has to do with the chasm that separates scientific from pre-scientific cultures. Wilson accepts the notion that myth and religion function like science to explain who we are and why we are here. But without the knowledge of natural sciences, humans are trapped in a cognitive prison. Science, in contrast to art and religion, the latter of which seeks to preserve mysteries, penetrates mystery in order to demonstrate the incredible order of a world shaped by natural selection. Wilson brings the same logic to the nature/ nurture controversy: both clearly are involved, and further research in genetics, on the one hand, and in psychology and sociology, on the other hand, will produce more precise allocations of nurture or nature situationally and perhaps even individually.

Finally, in this connection Wilson believes radically that Freud needs to be suspended as providing critical explanations of dreams and unconscious behavior until sufficient empirical research has been conducted to verify or nullify his views. The causes and treatment of schizophrenia, which have eluded many psychologists, seem to be amenable more to a genetic explanation and appropriate psychological treatment. Wilson is most tentative about the brain/mind duality. Wilson starts with the basic premise that "natural selection built the brain to survive in the world and only incidentally to understand it at a depth greater than is needed to survive" (*Consilience*, p. 66).

Humans thus share with all other creatures the survival thrust of the brain. But to master both survival and achieve dominance at a higher level—in effect to dominate the survival of all other creatures and the world of nature itself—the brain was compelled to create mind. That does not mean that the mind, or the intelligence gathering and analytical capacity of the mind, was fundamentally different physically, but rather neurophysically. In other words, mind was still a scientific engine, not a soul or spirit.

Indeed, current research needs to "to tighten the connectedness between the events and laws of nature, and the physical basis of human thought processes" (*Consilience*, p. 68). The molecular biology of the learning process will considerably enhance the study and creation of artificial intelligence as well as the embryonic field of artificial emotion.

Finally, Wilson believes that the three great areas of inquiry and convergence for the next twenty years will be mind, behavior, and ecology. Equally as important is the recognition that the ultimate goal of all science is "predictive synthesis," still in its infancy but extremely important and attainable. It is not achievable without enough empirically based demonstrations of consilience. But the substantial development of such evidence will be the emergence of predictive synthesis as the ultimate fruit of convergence.

What then are the yields of this examination of convergence as a megatrend? There at least five. The most obvious is that convergence has the capacity to radically disturb not merely the branches but the roots of all knowledge. Second, it is developmentally progressive and supports an epistemological and structural taxonomy not unlike Maslow's classic hierarchy. The following stages of evolution appear basic:

1. Similarity
2. Duality
3. Parallel
4. Paradox/Ambiguity

5. Crossovers
6. Integration
7. Synthesis
8. Convergence, Connexity, Consilience

Third, convergence provides the theoretical and empirical basis for understanding and anticipating a number of developments born of integration. These include the technology of theology; the creation of an internal pharmacy, brain chips, and the third intelligence; the appearance of the Great Convergence (the fusion of science and spirituality); and the pursuit of immortality.

Fourth, Mulgan took convergence into sociology, politics, and economics and envisioned interconnectedness as the antidote to excessive self-assertion by individuals and societies. His descriptions of the social benefits of connexity suggest that similar gains may be as possible and persuasive in the technological, scientific, and theological areas as well.

Finally, Edward O. Wilson offers resolutions to a number of the major debates of our time. In the process, he maintains that everything is linked, that nothing is singular, and ultimately that the physical, the spiritual, and cultural expressions of human existence and definition shall be known in common. It is a faith based on strong empirical research and documentation, and it represents his vision of the twenty-first century.

But if it is to happen with less rancor, the specialists need to become generalists and the generalists have to persuade the specialists to join them. The first step of convergence thus always requires exchange. The intermediate stage involves interdependence .The last step is always greater than the sum of all of the crossovers.

Chapter Thirteen

Future-Embedded Innovation Methodologies

All companies face the same problem of figuring out their future. Some may not already have in hand the target and the end game. They are still busy putting together the shape of the future beast. Uncertain of what it will be, they request data, study the competition, collect trends, estimate their capacity to shift focus, and so on.

Indirectly and often unintentionally, that process is diagnostic, in at least three ways. It provides an X-ray of how organizations think their way through to change, what options they characteristically identify, and finally what decision-making and planning protocols and systems they employ.

But often the problem with such complicated assessments is over-study. The more complex and elaborate, the more intimidating and overwhelming. Not surprisingly, refuge is sought in the form of tentative, partial, and contingent solutions. Even if the bull's eye is luckily hit, it is still accompanied and hedged by recommending further study and design. If the task were to build an ark, the engineers would be floating around with damp and incomplete plans in their hands.

But the problem is not solely one of commission. It is also fatally a sin of omission. And it is not solely a failure of action but of aspiration. Two up-scaling and indispensable dimensions are missing: first, requiring problem solving to also be innovation creating; second, shaping solutions that have at least one foot in the future.

Solutions should always invite the creative contribution of the future. They should not only be ahead of their present time and application, but also lure the future into this world and make it more available, earlier. Competitive edge or advantage thus may be redefined as access to the future, and innovation as the future incarnate. But wild brainstorming or imaginative overleaping cannot accomplish such solutions. What is still needed is one step at a time, slightly adjusted to follow five methodological guidelines.

First, the solutions-innovation-future search involves not just one but many steps. How many is unknown. Second, the steps can never be hurried or skipped. The biggest failing is stopping too soon or early in the game. It is equivalent to passing off the short as the long term. Third, the temptation is to settle prematurely for small gains. Timidity always argues for early arrival. It gives the illusion of engaging the future when in reality it is only an update. In short, the enemy of innovation is "incrementalism." Fourth, the final step can never be known in advance. As the classic job description puts it: whatever it takes to get the job done. It is unlike the classic Japanese system of asking "why" five times until one gets to the root cause: the precise number of steps is never specified. Fifth, the final step is signaled by its totality and durability. It must straddle both present and future; encompass the total problem posed, with no parts left out or over; and, finally, be able to live in this world and to be used by real people in real time and space.

The process itself as well as its final yield must always evidence a persuasive and retroactive logic. Previous steps are never discarded but cumulatively carried forward. Its ultimate end point is startling, unavoidable, and bold. The solution stands as if it is has always been there. It has an obvious and almost inevitable logic to it. It stands at the threshold of the future. Its presiding image is that of the two-faced Janus: retrospect and prospect.

How can this shift to next-step thinking/innovation best come about? The contention here is that it involves up-scaling and futurizing three commitments:

1. Mission: Innovation and learning as well as their kinship with each other have to become an integral and central part of organizational mission. Ideally, that double commitment should extend deep into the organization and embrace every employee by becoming a critical factor of employee and performance evaluation. Futuristic organizations in fact are characterized in two ways: first, by the inclusion of innovation in mission statements; and second, by the degree to which the company is innovation and knowledge oriented, directed, or driven. Indeed, the most driven often are associated with the commitment to corporate universities and the development of unique innovation methodologies, such as Six Sigma by GE. In a survey of the mission statements of 301 companies, the favorite words were "Quality, "Value," and "Service." Only 68 of the 301 listed innovation (Management First, 2003).

2. Futuristic: Solutions-oriented cultures rather than problem-oriented cultures always live ahead of their time. Their strategy is that of leapfrogging—while we are in the process of catching up let us also get

ahead. Enlightened leadership and companies also structure company-wide collaboration. They especially prize the contributions of mid-level mangers to the anticipatory process. Being proactive generates the inclusive energy of forward-looking management and leadership.

3. Holistic: Companies that get there first with the most and the best applications always carry forward, re-create, and project the big picture. They build arks that include all constituencies and address every contingency. The classic substitution is to settle for a piece and pass it off as a whole; or opt for an early solution that makes the task more manageable in present terms rather than a solution, which may be self-managing in future terms. Baby steps and obedient incrementalism limit visions and impoverish potential. In fact, it is precisely such piecemeal timidity that prematurely cuts off the present from the future, and forsakes innovation for incremental gains. Much of the power of all organizational future journeys derives in fact precisely from the emergence of new wholes that are shaped by that future.

In short, organizations that make innovation and learning part of their mission, and are holistically proactive, generate innovations that are designed in large part by and for the future. The test of the innovation is whether, minimally, it converges forecast and survival of the forecast and, optimally, positions itself for the next convergence and the next after that. The future has to be played like a step-by-step chess game in which every move prefigures and anticipates the next and the next. Chess mastery always involves multiple positioning. The endgame always exhibits the final logic of checkmate.

The following attention-getting opening line recently appeared in an ad by a major management consulting firm: "Traditional avenues to corporate growth are no longer available." To be sure, the firm, not unlike stock brokers, then engaged in persuasive semantic bait-and-switch substitutions as a way of still staying in the game. Clients and customers were then offered new solutions uniquely available in reassuring language.

Such cosmetic shell games are unfortunate for many obvious reasons. These are tough times and that truth needs to be told. Businesses in many ways are facing major and real impasses. Many of the obstacles are not temporary, partial, or occasional. If there are ways out, it may require companies turning themselves inside out (perhaps again). Above all, it will compel defining deficiencies not just in present but in future terms.

Are things really that bad? The ad did not lie. Here are ten short-term trends that sum up the first issue: double-digit growth is no longer likely; there may be limits to increasing productivity; manufacturing increasingly will be shifted overseas and the only offsetting American exports will be largely agricultural; short-term expedients have stripped the positioning and leveraging flexibility of many companies; mergers and acquisitions no longer attract investors; margins have become tighter; price increases often reduce market share; innovation cannot sufficiently offset glutted markets; even international expansion offers only limited opportunity and is accompanied now by higher risks; the stock market may not satisfy the search for investment, so alternative sources will be sought as fewer companies go public. In short, some believe businesses may be encountering not only the limits to growth, but also more seriously, the limits to the future.

But many will argue that such challenges have occurred before and have been weathered. There will be a general winnowing out of too many companies and of too many inept performers. Displaced workers will find other jobs. Competition seems to be solving the teacher shortage problem: unemployed engineers are now teaching high school math and science. In other words, the hidden hand of capitalism will muddle its often painful way through, and recovery and stability will be once more restored. Perhaps (although certainly at considerable costs in confidence and human dislocation).

But the larger issue is: Why have faith only in the power of external cycles over which we have little control? To be sure, we are proactive in other ways. We develop long-range forecasts and strategic plans, often industry specific; compile and inventory trends; employ expert methodologies to identify probability and impact; and undertake research and education in future studies. We even have developed a slogan of synthesis: "Think globally, act locally." But although it wisely combines and even occasionally aligns the macro and the micro, it omits a critical next step: "Implement internally."

What is generally lacking is the infusion of futures directly into business processes. The future already is environmentally active outside the gates of business. The next step is to go inside—into its everyday operations. If the future of the future is to become more manageable, it has to become more operational. Nor can it remain an abstract and vague gesture of vision; it needs to be wired directly in place.

Currently, the future is either an executive prerogative or an enclave of strategic planning and marketing. In either case, it is generally removed from basic operations. When strategic plans are rapidly implemented without prior consultation they often encounter negative feedback and even silent mutiny. Sometimes the response is so intense that the plan is sent back to the drawing board. The full and unexpected contributions of the future can only be tapped when the future functions not solely as an external values-added supplement but, rather, as an internal part of the way work is envisioned, organized, and done. Indeed, the degree to which that is embedded and granted an authentic voice defines how the future is valued.

THREE TYPES OF FUTURES BUSINESS

Organizations open to the future are of three types: mild, lukewarm, and hot. Mild companies are just future oriented. The future is generalized; it is more of an aura than a force. It is invoked in mission statements and adorns the walls of corporate training centers. Lukewarm companies are future directed. Their priorities are reflected in a mixture of detailed short-term plans ballasted and redeemed with vague midterm positioning. Strategic planning often neither exists as a separate division nor employs a separate staff. It is directed by the vice president of marketing and its strategies are determined, predictably, by market segmentation. Hot companies are future driven. The future is not an occasional but an obsessional and integral part of everything. It is not added on but embedded in virtually every process. As a result, it supports a companywide collective vision of collaborative and proactive leadership.

FUTURE-DRIVEN COMPANIES

How, then, does a company become future driven? What specific and generic business practices would benefit by being futures infused or amplified, and what would the benefits be? Here is a partial list:

Basic Practices	Futures Additions	Benefits
Decision Making	Anticipatory Perceptions	Tested in Advance
Communications	Values Advocate	Market Precision
Leadership	Decentralization	Distributed Leadership
Job Evaluation	Work Trends	Future-Focused Workforce
Strategic Planning	Employee Participation	Multiple & Diverse Forecasts
Problem Solving	Long-Term Solutions	Scenarios and Simulations

Using the above matrix as a guideline, how does one build and create a future-driven company?

Installing and incorporating futures additions is not a quick fix. In fact, it minimally involves two stages: review and refocusing. The first is total, the second aggregative.

Review (Total Process Analysis)

The application of futures should lead ultimately and ideally to a 360-degree review of all basic company processes. Initially, however, the focus may be limited and selective. But no matter where one starts the resistance to looking ahead is so regularly encountered that it becomes a given. Indeed, that is often only the tip of the proverbial iceberg when compared to how deep-seated and threatening the reluctance may be, and how surprising its causes.

For example, a discussion with supervisors about offering employees a more proactive exercise about work futures rapidly brought to the surface their views of workers in general. The supervisors believed that most employees lack the basic intelligence and even the self-worth to undertake such a task. Besides, they really prefer to be directed and are happier when told what to do. The same general devaluing response came from strategic planners, who raise similar objections about bottom-up planning and openly objected to what they perceived as a diminishment of their authority and the new jurisdiction and judgments of amateurs. Communications professionals withdrew from the challenge altogether. Although they conceded that many decisions at all levels were poorly conceived from a communications point of view, they were hesitant when offered the opportunity to become directly involved in the decision-making process itself. Most preferred to remain outside and after the process. They were content to wordsmith the results.

In short, the introductory review stage, though turbulent and often antagonistic, can generate four key clarifying heads-up guidelines: (1) The future is one thing, futurizing is another. The former is familiar, token, and generic, the latter invasive, unfamiliar, and threatening. (2) Bringing the proactive inside the house and making it an integral part of daily work and thought is routinely dislocating. (3) The prospect of future implementation often brings to the surface many unflattering and negative assumptions about the CEO, the company, workers, and its operations. The future functions like a magnet for dissension. (4) Encouraging the company and its workers to project what's ahead often generates fearful future prospects. General avoidance and even denial follow, and there is a return quickly to ostrich mentality.

But far from being discouraging, the review process confirms what many have found: namely, that the most important initial value of applying futures is diagnostic. Functioning as a comprehensive probe, the future is able to identify weak process links, negative assumptions, avoidance responses, absence of trust and collaboration, and past-oriented attitudes and practices. An array of failures and problems emerge across the board and from top to bottom. Somehow the future acts as a holistic X-ray exposing the weak links of the total organization.

Refocusing (Integrating the Horizontal and the Vertical)

One of the values of reviewing basic operations is that they are redundant at all levels throughout the company. A typically more popular and even glamorous approach would be to restrict attention to top leadership. But that goes counter to what future diagnosis and reconfiguration reveals.

Leadership is no longer singular but multiple, not dominating but distributed, not downward but a two-way street. Similarly, determining the future and its training agenda are no longer the monopoly of strategic planning or human resources but become a collective, companywide participatory and anticipatory effort. The full extent of futurizing thus requires aggregation.

To avoid piecemeal, partial, or lower levels of comprehension and achievement it is critical that the processes that have been reconfigured with a built-in futures component be aggregated upward to help define companywide levels and optimums. What emerges are generally higher-level bell curves of performance than previously achieved. The performance level of all rises. In addition, a shared vision of future directions and the training agenda required to get there emerges as the product of shared purpose.

By tapping horizontal process yields across the board, and directing their definition and application increasingly upward, companies can achieve a double alignment: in the present and in the future. Company needs can now be directly engaged by prioritizing and aligning current and future performance goals with current and future company goals. In addition, the company enjoys the benefits not only of a collective vision of the future, but also the reconfigured means of getting there.

Typically, such double gains characterize future-driven organizations. But they do not come easily or quickly. The diagnostic future is often perceived as an enemy not an ally. The refocused future threatens assured roles and invades comfort zones. CEOs and senior staff especially feel undermined by calls for collective and distributed rather than charismatic leadership.

Although the opposition may be formidable, the gains more than offset the difficulty. Beyond achieving improvements of productivity, profitability and quality, future-driven companies also may pursue three future ideals: the transformation of organizations into communities, the renegotiation of worker contracts into worker covenants, and the redirection of futures application from external forecasts to internal reconfigurations and refocusing of basic business processes.

Such a composite would then define future-driven organizations as collaborative communities of best practices designed to survive a tough present, and structured to achieve its own defined and preferred future. Turned outwardly, that may provide just the competitive advantage business needs. Turned inwardly it may provide the vision to conceive of and create the workforce of the future. But what is that?

Not too long ago the employee virtues that Human Resources (HR) extolled and recruited for were being dutiful, hardworking, trustworthy, loyal, and obedient. Those past-oriented attributes now have been supplemented by a new crop of present-focused behaviors: adaptability, involvement, agility, innovation, ownership, transformation, mutuality, alignment, morale, and empowerment. Finally, future-driven qualities have appeared or are emerging: knowledge worker, team player, customer-advocate, technologically amplified and distributed leader.

The range of the above characteristics of past-oriented to present-focused to future-driven employees has been structured by a thirty-year process of structural redistribution and reengineering: the gradual flattening of the organizational pyramid that conferred upon managers prerogatives and responsibilities previously reserved for senior officers, and, in turn, employee empowerment assumed from mid-level managers more control and self-direction. In short, decentralization not concentration became the order of the day and even of the future.

The new centrality of employees proceeded from the recognition that if productivity, profitability, and creativity were to occur and provide the competitive edge in a global marketplace, the base of the now nearly flat pyramid was where it would be found. Indeed, in some organizations teams have either replaced or made marginal their supervisors. The task of HR was to keep pace with those changes and above all to help deliver and train employees in the new elements of each ethos as they in turn were altered to minister to new challenges.

But in many ways and areas, HR needs to push the envelope of worker knowledge further by gaining more information about how workers in fact acquire knowledge. In particular, research recently has focused on the demographics of the workforce and what that reveals about the sociology and psychology of their leadership and learning preferences.

Demographics

As already noted, in a large corporations at least five typically (soon to be six) generations coexist. The oldest were born in the fifties, the newest in the eighties. The first group probably will live until 2050, the second almost to 2100.

The past and future histories of those generations often determine their work attitudes, preferences, and behaviors. The degree to which they are willing to work together in turn affects the degree of alignment with company goals. In an e-commerce start-up, all are usually the same generation. That is why they can move so far so fast. Differentiation is not an obstacle because it is minimal. But that is also why many fail. There is no internal tension, and diversity is not sufficiently present or able to exhibit its checks and balances.

Targeted Behaviors

The complexity of multiple generations and behaviors has become an object for greater study. We are beginning to know much more about why employees do and do not do certain things. The process requires keeping three targets in sight at the same time: (1) identifying targeted behaviors desired by HR and the company (usually drawn from one or a combination of those on the above lists), (2) determining what in the employee's demographics and background supports or opposes that change—a series of diagnostic overlays registers inertia or flow—and (3) identifying the bridging forces, methodologies, and strategies of coaches to win or bring them over to the desired side.

Such a process would be daunting if it had to done every time for every behavior for every employee. But the diagnostic middle piece noted above once done is stored in a database and can be tapped again when the targeted behaviors change. The task also has been eased by a deeper understanding of employee-manager relationships.

Employee Preferences

A typical continuum of leadership styles would include the following: the autocratic, benevolent autocratic, consultative, and participative. Others have condensed the categories to two: directive and non-directive leadership and coaching styles; and then noted the following characteristics of each:

Directive	Non-Directive
Power-shift cultures	Achievement-oriented cultures
Role-oriented cultures	Support-oriented cultures
Rules	Goals
Roles	Innovation

To this must be added how worker differences affect the perceptions of the above managerial styles. The findings appear in the eight categories listed below. In effect, these factors constitute the basic demographics of all employees, but focus on identifying potential support for or obstacles to change:

Age
Gender
Nationality
Education level
Tenure with organization
Functional area
Hierarchical level.
First born, middle, last-born.

Here are Hofstede's (1997) interpretations of each factor on the list as it bears on leadership style preferences.

Age

Generally older workers prefer and respond to directive managerial and coaching styles. Younger workers respond better to non-directive coaches and managers. Some high-tech starts-ups where all employees are in their twenties show a high tolerance for chaos and even anarchy.

Gender

Males prefer directive styles, women non-directive. Typically, men are more forceful and assertive, women more cooperative and nurturing. Increasingly, however, convergence is occurring, although women may be leading the way there.

Nationality

National cultures shape citizens' leadership preferences. Strong and assertive national cultures want strong leaders. Other more egalitarian countries in fact distrust leaders having too much power, and favor imposing constitutional limits on executive power.

Educational level

Typically the higher the level of education the greater the inclination to favor the non-directive leadership style.

Tenure with Organization

The longer the period of employment, the greater reliance on directive leadership; although if there have been a succession of poor or mediocre CEOs, the allegiance may be accompanied by skepticism.

Functional area

Predictably, blue-collar employees favors strong bosses, white collar employees more non-directive ones.

Hierarchical Level

Line personnel and managers favor what they are and increasingly want to become. Staff want an easier life associated with simply being told what to do.

Birth Order

First born tend to be more aggressive and insecure, and more resistant to authority. Last born are more distant and harder to reach, and often capricious. The middle are usually the most reasonable, although they can lean on occasion toward the behaviors of the first and last and sometimes both at the same time.

The next step is to compile a demographic cluster, which provides guidelines as to the key perceptions and attitudes of the employee being managed or coached. Consider the example of two sample employees. One is an older director of the transportation division whose general profile places him a directive cluster. That is followed by a younger employee who leads a team of mostly entry-level software engineers and who falls within a non-directive cluster.

What does such clustering offer leaders of innovation? The first pattern shows instances of initiatives being taken over by employees correlated with a partiality to a non-directive leadership style or a lack of initiative as a result of having to relate to a highly directive manager. Another finding is that employees who prefer a non-directive style are more open and responsive to questions about different and even more creative ways of doing their job. In contrast, employees who prefer doing what they are told will be more reluctant to volunteer suggestions for change or improvement and prefer instead to have the coach tell them what they should be doing differently.

For companies that develop a future stance in which work performance has to be continuously improved, innovation encouraged, and teaming a new norm, the role of the leader is to become that of a stretch agent. His task is not only to coach change, but also to align and wire it in place in terms of specific job requirements and expectations, on the one hand, and company objectives on the other.

With an expanded demographic and knowledge base accompanied by the many clusters that it can generate and sustain, the leader-coach has a richer and more diverse and flexible set of alternative routes to take. In fact, taking the time to provide employees with an opportunity to share their histories, perspectives, values, and the overall complexities of their lives and work sets the stage often for affecting change and job improvement.

Both leader and employees have a great deal to contribute and to learn from such exchanges. Such equality and mutuality hopefully generates a tangible model of what future work relationships should be all about. Turnaround of employees requires the combination of art and science. Databases and demographic clusters set up the science; the coach functions as a knowledge artist. The dynamic dialogue of partnership between equals raises the task of integrating performance and change to a new level for HR professionals. Performance evaluation that combines the science of data and art of partnerships may provide employees and managers with the greatest challenge each has ever faced

An unusual but critical area that tests futurists is finding leaders with foresight, often early on before their reputations are made. Would Jack

Welch or Bill Gates have been tagged when they were still young and virtually unknown? It is a particularly appropriate task for futurists because of the
need to identify leaders for a different future. It thus requires always a double
knowledge: an early leadership detection system coupled with scenarios of
what will be required of leaders in the future.

But why is that important? Changing challenges shape the job profile.
They may even prescribe a global and interdisciplinary range. Organizations
have to become increasingly self-conscious about anticipatory leadership development. (If leaders are made, not born, then the company needs to study
how best they can be made. If leaders are born, not made, then the company
needs to know what those genetic qualities are. Besides, even the born are
made somewhat.) Such knowledge benefits the embryonic leader. It makes
him or her more self-conscious about planning and designing a future professional life. They have to write a career script. Their life becomes crafted.
They may have to become, in turn, futurists.

Although knowledge about what defines a future leader can come from
many sources, some employ alternative routes. As noted previously, for
many years I served as an executive coach and trusted advisor to CEOs and
senior staff. Not unexpectedly, the subject of the future and above all the
characteristics of future leaders were a recurrent subject. Three occasions
triggered dialogue: (1) identifying and advancing future leaders in their organization or those in their competitor's and how to lure them away; (2)
finding a successor to the throne or new member of the board or senior
cabinet; (3) conducting especially for a captive audience of senior staff an
endless and open-ended seminar on the characteristics and qualities of
emerging leadership.

As a group these CEOs were uniquely wise, cynical, egotistical, and
cocksure. They believed they had a monopoly on the knowledge of the
future. No one could or would contest their pontification. To their credit,
however, these executives were always insightful, so much so that in my
judgment their seminars were far superior to most offered at doctoral programs in business. More to the point, there was remarkable agreement as to
what makes or breaks emerging leaders for a changing future. Here then are
the five common denominators for identifying future leaders:

1. vision: the big picture now and ahead
2. mission: leadership sharing
3. operations: transparent excellence and flawless execution
4. structure: decentralized and collaborative
5. commitment to professional development: unlearning and transition
    training

Before elaborating on them, the discussion needs minimally to be framed and a futures context needs to be identified for each of the five categories. That preserves the role of the future as a partner in identifying the characteristics and qualities of leadership. Indeed, in many ways, objections might be made that these five leadership qualities do not appear very futuristic. In fact, they seem quite traditional. Not so, however, when the future bears down on them and alters both their form and content. The following matrix provides futures equivalents for each and will be folded into the discussion of how those futures dimensions challenge, drive, and shape the emerging leader.

Leadership Qualities	*Their Futures Context*
Vision:	Interdependent World
Mission:	Collaborative and Holistic Decision Making
Operations:	Horizontal Congruence and Vertical Alignment
Structure:	Employee Centrality
Professional Development:	Unlearning

PROFILES OF FUTURE LEADERS

Vision

Generally, the contemporary discussion of vision has been muted or minimized. It appears as too grandiose and of an earlier time when major enterprises were launched. The days when Walt Disney could stand on a mound and look over acres of swampy land are over. No new big companies will be created. Anything new is really variations or combinations on what already existed. And so vision is disposed of and subsumed under mission, especially by those hard-nosed types who do not wish to be deflected form dealing with real stuff by puffery.

But acknowledging the future in fact restores vision to the agenda. One of the functions of the future, especially a compelling and discontinuous future, is to disturb the present. Consider the projection of the two spikes alone, in technology and population. Can any organization not find its mission jarred or rendered askew? When such shocks to the system occur, only vision can serve to restate what lies ahead and how we engage it. Mission then takes its obedient second place in the pecking order.

The major new factor of vision is globalization. As a system, it is denser and more elusive than we realized. It generates strange or different partnerships: software companies subcontracting with programmers in India, manufacturers exporting the most polluting stages of their process, epidemics crossing national and even international lines, and so on. In other words, the increasing interconnectedness of the world compels a vision, which seeks to comprehend, express, and somehow master the new competence of interdependence. Moreover, in scale and daring such an effort would be not unlike the impressive one a number of years ago by Meadows and Forester in *The Limits to Growth*.

Meadows and Forrester were visionary futurists. Their computer simulation model, while flawed (it had to be), nevertheless produced a powerful finding: there is no human goal that requires more people to achieve it. Their study itself had all the impact of the future. Critics found fault with their databases, with the lines of interacting factors, with the entire computer model. Nevertheless, the impact was so great that reviewers in their discussion even changed the focus from the "limits to growth" to the "end of growth." Ideologically, for many the limits to growth meant the end of growth. And so systematically we shot (down) the messengers and gave global visionary efforts a bad name for quite a while.

Effective future leaders have to build a series of new visions of the planet, its relations to the environment and to each other (perhaps they should be the same), to sustainable growth and redistribution, and above all to the complex and often fragile ways the new globalism operates. Those new leaders have to assemble and peruse a new futures bibliography, which focuses on the kind of span of Meadows and Forester and many others, on the one hand, and the imaginative range of the science fictionists, on the other hand.

Finally, the parameters of the vision must go beyond obvious self-interest. It should not follow the old pattern of accumulating a fortune, perhaps rapaciously, and then spending the twilight years dispensing wisdom as George Soros recently and interestingly has been doing or creating a foundation to dispense largesse and cleanse guilt posthumously. Rather, the vision should address not only global economics but political science so as to preserve the option that leaders may exercise, as part of a larger cumulative and reinforcing effort, the building of a sustainable future. The future cannot be left to governments especially dreadful ones and their notions of national security and sovereignty. A new dialogue has to include visionary leaders whose principal agenda item is always the future of the planet.

Mission

Ideally, each leadership characteristic should somehow resonate with all the others. The effort, however, should not compel a stifling consistency but rather demonstrate that future leadership has an interlocking range, that it is conceived, reflected on, and adjusted to be coherently whole. In this way, the most insistent dimension of the future, global interdependence, impacts on all the characteristics of leadership.

Thus, the mission of the leader is no longer a separatist entity designed to serve only those who lead. Nor is it solely limited to how the CEO can best lead his company. The future compels a new consideration: What do I do with my leadership? How do I use it? Traditionally, leadership belonged exclusively to those at the top. It was held close. It was a source of power and distinction. If it sought change, it was in the form of how to exercise more power over more holdings. Leaders of old always were empire builders and inevitably monopolists. Their goal like empire builders was to extend their rule totally.

Future leaders are not timid or myopic. They know that the top holds power and sway. But the new futures issue is how the power of the leader is leveraged. How can it be used to meet organizational change on the one hand and global change on the other? In other words, leadership has joined intellectual capital as a major factor on the asset side of the ledger. Leadership itself is on the block. How leaders use the assets of leadership determines whether the company succeeds and in fact has a future. The key mission, then, of futuristic leaders is leadership transfer and sharing in order to encourage and preserve the possibility that each leadership initiative could be aggregated upward and potentially be applied companywide.

Operations

According to Peter Drucker, Warren Bennis, Tom Peters, and many other leadership gurus, the overriding distinction of outstanding leaders is their decisiveness. They are able to make decisions within tight time frames, often with less than total data at their command, and choose a course from among a bewildering and complex set of options. That ability alone, all claim, sets apart the men from the boys, the successful leaders from the wanna-bes.

But leaders of and shaped by the future will need to be not only more decisive, but also technologically assisted and amplified. Increasingly, real and just-in-time data systems provide access and transparency to virtually all operations. In some cases the data will make the decision or more will be asked for such an automatic process to take place. The role of the leader will shift from content to context. Futurity and globalism may be joined at the hip.

Structure

Currently, success or profitability is determined by productivity, quality, and customer satisfaction. The future factor is innovation. It is the CEO's task to insure the interlocking durability of all factors. And in the past that was exclusively perceived as in fact the responsibility of leadership, at the top and throughout the middle.

Embracing distributed leadership brought a degree of decentralization that was immediately bracing and productive. Decisions could be made quickly on the micro-operational level without having to endure the time delay of ascending the chain of command. The introduction of new technology also often impacted productivity. But the global competition, especially impelled by much lower wages and standards of living, became crushing. To survive, leaders had once again to use their leadership in a unique way.

Gradually, over time employee productivity began to supplement technological productivity; employee centrality began to extend distributed leadership. Leadership transferred its capital once more, but this time more radically and created a new governance structure: the employee collaborative.

The process was gradual, even piecemeal, because few leaders foresaw the prospect of employee leadership in totality and because the evidence was not in that, in fact, it would work. But the latest and numerically the most extensive decentralization created a major supplement to distributed leadership in the form of new collaborative governance structure. Employees gradually in terms of governance were brought from the periphery to the center, from being the objects to being the subjects of productivity, from being workers to being partners. This newest investment of leadership capital was again driven by global competition, in particular the lower wages and standards of living of competitors. Technology alone could not offset the differential (in some cases it even increased it). Only employee productivity could even the odds.

Thus new structural norms began to appear: teams became the dominant form of work relationships; quality and productivity employee circles were charged with producing time and cost-saving changes; alignment teams were created across divisional lines to achieve a double alignment, horizontal and vertical, and thus to bring divisional goals and company goals in line; planning and scheduling even of projected layoffs became increasingly an employee responsibility; evaluation factored in more heavily employee self-evaluation and a 360-degree perspective to bring customers into the heart of the process; employees increasingly had input into the training agenda, often creating unofficial employee universities when they also were asked to serve as workshop instructors; and most recently, depending upon the enlightenment or desperation of the company involved, employees have been invited to be involved in futures scanning processes.

In the process of discussing this empowerment of workers as stakeholders, one older retired CEO remarked, "If we had been smart enough to do all this earlier, we might have avoided unions." That sparked a lively exchange between us, which included the observation that the union take on employee centrality might be 180 degrees away from his but, more to the point, neither position was a leadership one. Taking the high visionary road, what set leaders apart is the degree to which they accept the future as the determining and defining ideology. And what the future offers is the prospect of a collaborative governance structure that requires not only leadership vision of its value, but also willingness to make an incredible investment of leadership capital into the hands of workers. Perhaps the most dramatic example has occurred in the form of an employee environmental scanning process in which teams or divisions read, identify, and discuss trends and rate and record their durability and degree of impact on a monthly trending form. The forms are aggregated upward and reissued with common denominators identified. That establishes companywide commonality to identify leadership options. What more could a futuristic CEO ask?

Professional Development

Typically, professional development is sporadically driven by the budget and its agenda is determined by the top or supervisors. Although one of the new yields of the collaborative governance structure is the increasing acceptance of employee input, what about the professional development of leaders?

Typically, they are exempt or removed from the process. To be sure, they may decide what the training should be or serve as cheerleaders for Senge's learning organization, but generally they generate the questionable image that they are complete. They have achieved perfection, otherwise they would not be where they are. But one of the telltale signs distinguishing present-occupied from future driven-leaders is that the latter model their incompleteness and the need for lifelong learning and development.

In particular, futuristic leaders have to embrace and promulgate minimally three kinds of professional development: futuristics, holistics, and innovation. As noted, future leaders need to study the future of the future. In every communication CEOs in one form or other must share news of and from the future. One CEO I know who was passionate about science fiction created and extraterrestrial newsletter.

Holistics is a critical antidote for companies too preoccupied with incremental development, just as unlearning is the threshold for innovation. It falls to the leader who openly, officially, and frequently describes the ways in which unexamined past assumptions have blocked ways of thinking outside the box. That is best done, as I have witnessed it, by leaders telling stories of their own mistakes, opacity, myopia, and misplaced priorities. They become learning leaders by paradoxically advocating unlearning.

Chapter Fourteen

The New Species of Boxes—Think Yourself Out of Those!

We often and glibly call for thinking outside the box based on two mistaken assumptions: that all boxes are the same and that the same kind of thinking will work in all cases. Indeed, we act as if both are generic—that one size fits all. No wonder why the proposed solutions are not much better than what they replaced and there are so few examples of successful extrication. In short, we have failed to provide tough guidelines to give our champions of innovative thinking a fighting chance. Below are five such basic correctives to even the odds:

Size: Boxes come in different sizes—small, medium, large, extra-large and extra-extra-large. The obvious correlation is not only to numbers but also to company diversity. When both are extended by international holdings and operations, then size scaled, layered, and differentiated also becomes a source of its demographic secrets and its known and unknown variables. The first step, then, is always dimensional—arriving at the heft of its weight and substance; otherwise, we would be without the tough standards to guide and judge whether the solution is the right fit.

History: Is it an old or a new box? Have we kept a record of our failures? Has it changed in any way since it first surfaced? From what to what? And why then? Is it collective? Rooted in the momentum of custom or habit? (This is the way we have operated and solved problems for years!) Or more obstinate, buried in the culture of turf management and become also inevitably political as well? Most serious, has it hardened and been promulgated as policy?

Urgency: Is it an occasional itch, a recurrent pain in the neck? Or a chronic condition? Temporary or terminal? Its impact? Manageable—we are still limping along, with labored breathing at the third quarter but forecasts are we are running out of time, losing the innovation race, and unable to attract and keep new talent. For some strange reason, when the word gets out that we don't ourselves think outside the box very often, candidates shun us.

Marshaling in-house creative sources: The value of calling for thinkers outside the box is that it dramatizes the range of creative sources available for the company to tap. But who typically surfaces? R&D types, past successful thinkers, generally the same old hands. The result is that you often come up short. That is followed by the embarrassing recognition that you should have been proactive—that nothing has been done across the board to develop in advance a new core of outside-the-box-thinkers. They do not just happen or appear. They have to be the result of a conscious program of building creativity.

Experimental: In addition to building internal innovative capacity, a thinking lab has to be established to experiment with alternative thinking. That commitment in turn rests on the premise that some current boxes and many coming down the pike may elude standard current problem-solving tool kits. Other boxes house a 250-pound gorilla who resists being caught or caged. A few are freakish and appear to have come from outer space. In short, the species of boxes has changed so much so that the traditional solo approach may have to shift to a team approach of collaborative problem solving.

For bosses to call for thinkers outside the box and then walk away and leave it there signifies their own failure to think about box preparation, and about making the study and classifications of boxes part and parcel of the solution. In short, we need to acknowledge the extent to which we in turn are routinely contained and brainwashed by our work cubicles, and that our thinking itself is rigid and boxed. Acknowledging also that not all boxes are the same and that a new species of box increasingly will confront us offers the promise that the boxes we have to finally exceed will simultaneously be a form of self-liberation as well.

Chapter Fifteen

The Policy Box

We are so obsessed with getting everyone to think outside of the box that we have failed to ask some basic questions. Are all boxes the same and therefore requiring the same effort to escape? How many different kinds of boxes are there? Does a taxonomy exist? Not all boxes have the same holding power—some even putting obstacles to prevent breaking free. Finally, strange as it may seem to go-getters, many boxes are happy boxes, many professionals prosper and do good work there, promotions come regularly and fairly. Why leave when you don't know what awaits on the other side?

Hopefully, such misgivings above should slow down or make the urgent requests to think outside the box more discriminating, less hurried, and less mechanical. Meanwhile, it might be instructive to provide an example of the typical box inquiry process.

One of the most difficult boxes to crack is the policy box. Why? What is there about codified policy that makes it so tenacious—that holds on and resists creative reformulation?

Indeed, the first step is to acknowledge the extent of the box's resistance, even its irrational obstinacy and to ask some tough questions: Why do we have this stupid policy in the first place? What is its history? What were the original crafters so worried about that it could result in such a desperate solution? And how did it ever get approved?

Let us take one troublesome policy—extra charges on hotel bills—and run the film backwards. The chair of the policy committee calls a meeting. He begins, "We are getting a lot of negative feedback from customers about the extra charges we put on hotel bills two months ago. Equally upset are our customer reps, who, lacking an official policy, do not know how to respond."

Harry: "Couldn't they come up with some response on their own? What happened to good old creative initiative—especially from those who are supposed to be our customer experts?"

Don: "Why did we not anticipate the trouble and develop a policy in advance?"

Chair: "We hoped it would go under the radar, or if it did not, would ride home free on the coat tails of charging of extra baggage fees by the airlines."

Chuck: "Well clearly it did not work. So let us get down to the nitty-gritty and find out what kind of beast we've let loose and now have to rein back in."

Don: "I may be able to answer that at least in part. Three situations converged: the marketing decision to list rooms online with discounts to increase occupancy but it did not generate enough to offset revenue loss from lower priced rooms—producing a revenue gap. The second situation was all the acquisitions and mergers of hotels—ours included—into larger chains and the unexpected costs of consolidation. Finally the CEO and the board approaching a lackluster quarterly report period called for ways to increase profits substantially and quickly."

Chuck: "In other words, let us call a shovel a spade: we padded the bill. We figured how much was needed and packed it all into those phony charges. And we thought that questionable practice would not be challenged and we could continue to charge whatever the traffic could bear and get away with it."

Chair: Now wait a minute, Chuck."

Chuck: "OK, OK, I'm not getting on my high horse. But I think we've been caught with both hands in the cookie jar. I am not surprised by our naked greed—we are not the first and probably will not be the last. Meanwhile I do not envy those customer reps."

Don: "Exactly. But we do have to come up with a defensible policy they can use. What are our options?"

Chair: "Two tries. We first went through each of the charges to see if we could find a way to justify their inclusion but found that they were mostly untruthful or lame. The scenario accompanying this approach showed customers' responses to be angry and often out of control. Another approach was to suggest that this was increasingly a customary way of doing business, citing the airlines. That backfired, because all that did was double the anger but this time on our head. And that was as far as we went and where we are right now.

Don: "I'm not surprised. Any suggestions from the field?"

Chair:" Not a one except get rid of this flagrant red flag. Most of them have thrown up their hands in despair."

The committee brooded to no avail. Finally they agree to meet next week, consulting in the meantime with members of their departments for new ideas. The chair volunteered to see what research existed on the problem.

The committee reconvened, but all were in a foul mood. It seemed the time away and especially the consultations with colleagues had only soured the whole affair more. People were very angry that this was done in the first place and that it became their job to clean up the mess and defend the indefensible.

No one was willing to talk. No one had anything to say. The mood was one of surrender. Let another group be called to untie this Gordian knot. Then, unexpectedly, Chuck raised his weary hand to speak: "I move that the following be our policy for these additions to the bill: "I am sorry sir/madam but this is our policy."

Initially, all were startled. But, reflecting on the fact that all other ways seem blocked, agreement by exhaustion and desperation carried the day; and the policy was approved . . . unanimously.

That was not only failing to think outside the box. It pushed thinking back and deeper into the box and made thing less accessible and rationally reachable. It also created a box that by being shameful and counterproductive further turned away even the most competent and ethical practitioners of the art.

Chapter Sixteen

Advocates for Innovation

The new like the young are heady, assertive, and arrogant. The new seeks to be free of its origins, to exist independently on its own, without any debts or obligations of continuity. Enormously powerful, innovation can end old businesses, create new ones, impart new life to current ones—any or all of the above at any or all times. The old dilemma of how to stir such creative upstarts is thus accompanied and compounded by the new fear that it will be an ingrate and bite the hand that feeds it. Innovative outcomes are thus always a mix of new starts and end–games. But acknowledging and managing such ambiguity and yet still remaining committed to creating an innovative culture are not familiar operating assumptions of leadership.

Who at the top is the principal advocate of innovation? CEOs typically traffic in visions. They invoke the glories of what once was and/or what can be. Often cheerleaders, they call upon all to rise to the new occasion of saving the company by regaining its previous position and market share. But then what kind of leadership do the members of the executive team provide? Does the CLO, CFO, COO, and so on generate any separate messages of his or her own? Or is alignment so absolute and demanding that they are all obedient echoes? Is their difference subdued by the triumph of chain of command? But what if the unique leadership options of each discipline area were to emerge? Would they all be the same? To the point here, what would CLOs choose?

Although the workforce training challenges are many, five factors lead to innovation as the CLO's top choice. First, it is linked to vision. Indeed by inhabiting the same ground as the CEO, creativity minimally and persuasively reinforces his focus on futurity. Second, it is big picture. Innovation can lead the charge because it is macro-worthy—it inhabits the pantheon. Third, it is across the board. It thus offers the unity of common commitment and thereby the potential of serving as an inclusive company culture. Fourth, innovation is pivotal. It is the epitome of transformation. As such it emblems change for all. Finally, it sustains a new partnership between the incremental and the disruptive. It thus introduces such doubleness as a twenty-first=century training norm.

But nomination alone may not be sufficient to carry the day. To be accepted, the factors that elevate innovation above all other competing claims need a persuasive vehicle and context that accommodates and matches its leadership factors. In other words, a double argument is needed: to identify the forces that traditionally and recurrently shape and reshape vision and then introduce and position innovation as the central driver of a new worldview. Thus from the outset the beginnings and ends of creativity have to be linked to the same ambiguous interplay of vision. In addition, innovation and vision so paired cannot be ordered or commanded to emerge. They have to be coached, even teased out. Their commonality indeed should be a surprise. In short, it is the outcome not of action but reflection—of stepping back, pausing, and taking in the whole—contemplating the forces of origins and ends.

Such shaping of the new big picture should not be a deliverable already predigested or predetermined but an exploration of what is seminal and recurrent. CLOs thus have to develop exploratory model seminars focused on vision and innovation. The initial one would be led by and for the executive team. Then it would be adapted for general workforce application. A special adaptation would then become the orientation program for new hires.

What would be the content? Although the essentials of vision vary, its basic components always possess the recurrent and classic nature and behaviors of archetypes. The following five, it can be argued, have both the resiliency and pliability to be constant yet redefinable, and to sustain the illustrative examples that accompany each one: the new idea, systems, foresight, ideology, and leadership.

1. The New Idea!

Ideas are still civilization's most powerful mind-altering drug. Whether used as a lens to see the world in a new light or as an instance of discovery and insight—"I have an idea!"—big ideas not only shape the big picture but also contain embryonically its yet-to-be discovered versions. Conceptual nominations can range from the new globality in which the world is of a piece economically and ecologically or that it is now a flat and endlessly proliferating network; or both But in all instances the test is the power of re-conception to see doubly— to bridge the then with the now, and the now with the future. By seeking to close if not eliminate the gap between continuity and change, ideas function as the eternal version of a work in progress.

2. Systems

Systems are secrets connected by purpose. Although their patterns of meaning and relationship typically may operate beneath the surface even at great depth, when discovered, displayed and tracked they prove to be startlingly verifiable and unifying. The focus of archetypal system inquiry is thus always two fold. First, can all that is emerging fit in and be absorbed by existing paradigms? Or can such organizing systems be revised or redefined to facilitate accommodation? Failing that are there new systems or ecologies which have the maternal inclusiveness to accept and mother a new brood of those who do not look alike and are contentiously independent? But lest the nominating process be indulgent, all new or redefined archetypes must be systemic.

3. Foresight

Although looking ahead should be common to all archetypal
    inquiry, for foresight to be genuine and brave it must abandon the predictability of extrapolation and systematically focus instead on the disruptive. What's new must give way to what's next. In other words, strategic planners not only have to become futurists, but also embrace both that profession's reading and techniques of the laws and behaviors of discontinuous futures. Such anticipatory specialists over five decades have developed the expertise to see the future as a transparent enigma worthy of archetypal status.

4. Ideology

All forecasts are three-fold. They identify the probable (most likely), the possible (including wild cards) and the preferable (what is hoped for). It is the last that offers the prospect or illusion of control and purpose. and that always has constituted the ideology of archetypes. The mediation between traditional and new values thus is potentially directive and promises the exoneration of justification. But as with all reviewed and redefined archetypes, the outcomes must be totally inclusive, capable of diverse consensus and futuristically sustainable. In other words, ideology of all considerations invokes and applies its parallel partners to discipline its own quest. Otherwise ideology will render all aspiration as partisan and based on exclusivity. My keys to heaven should not lock you out.

5. Leadership

Who is in charge and who decisively chooses what future to pursue obviously belongs in the pantheon of archetypes. Indeed, of all the eternal verities this one is the most popular probably because it is adored, even worshiped. It has spawned an endless series of best sellers, motivational speakers, and leadership gurus in all ages, in all cultures. But unlike its archetypal companions it not only has long life and persistence of its own, but also borders on the sacred and the eternal. To be sure, although each period addresses and offers many new and endless variations on the theme of the savior, few if any contemplate (as is routinely done with all the other archetypes) the radical prospects of its coming to an end or being so transformed that it longer bears any real and substantial resemblance to its predecessors. In other words, because of its mesmerizing difference and sacred hold the subject of leadership epitomizes not only the difficulty of revisiting and revising, but also the danger of archetypes becoming stereotypes. In short, access has to begin and end with who leads; and why leaders have been deemed to be so needed even as necessary evils.

Such a daunting exercise inevitably leads to the reassuring question: Who else is undertaking such quixotic ventures? Sadly, no one has a major effort or program under way. But then at least it must be occurring in the academy? It sounds like their kind of pie-in the-sky inquiry. Not as a mainstream pursuit. Actually, there are some affirmative examples, but they are not found in conventional forms and thus provide a further understanding of the off-center nature of archetypal review. For example although often announced with limited focus so as to attract single-minded practitioners, new and future versions of archetypes frequently appear in conferences and symposia. Then too, although often absent from the standard curriculum, the activity of satellite research centers and divisions almost clandestinely is archetypally driven. In other words, not unexpectedly the cutting edge is at the periphery, the future emerges with upstarts and start-ups, and innovation is a minority voice disturbing the universe.

The task of training is thus sequentially multiple. It must initially preside over three transformations: imagining the familiar, then imagining the unimaginable, and finally imaginative managing of the manageable. In the process, it has to structure the emergence of the future, but one that offers the comfort of at least a familiar alien from outer space who nevertheless speaks the basic language of archetypes.

www.ingramcontent.com/pod-product-compliance
Lightning Source LLC
Chambersburg PA
CBHW021821270326
41932CB00007B/288